(fiche)

AN OUTLINE OF
MIDDLE ENGLISH GRAMMAR

AN OUTLINE OF
MIDDLE ENGLISH
GRAMMAR

by Karl Brunner
Emeritus Professor, University of Innsbruck

translated by

Grahame Johnston
Professor, University of Melbourne

OXFORD
BASIL BLACKWELL
1965

© in this translation 1963
BASIL BLACKWELL

First Printed 1963
Reprinted 1965

Translated from the Fifth Edition of
Abriss der mittelenglischen Grammatik
(MAX NIEMEYER VERLAG, TÜBINGEN)

Printed in Great Britain by
Robert Cunningham and Sons Ltd.
Alva, Scotland

CONTENTS

TRANSLATOR'S NOTE

This book is a translation of the fifth edition of Professor Karl Brunner's *Abriss der mittelenglischen Grammatik* (Max Niemeyer Verlag, Tübingen, 1962). Some changes of presentation and notation have been made, but in other respects my aim has been to make available to English-speaking students of our early literature a faithful version of a textbook which has proved its value to a generation of German students. In my experience, the clarity and conciseness of Professor Brunner's outline make it particularly suitable for first- and second-year university students, and of help to their seniors.

The technical terms used in the translation are those in common use. It is perhaps worth remarking, however, that 'initially', 'medially' and 'finally' always have the sense 'at the beginning', 'in the middle', and 'at the end' of a word or syllable.

I am grateful to the author and his original publisher for their ready consent to the appearance of an English version, to Mr H. L. Schollick of Blackwell's for his advice, and to my colleague Miss M. Bouquet for invaluable help with the translation.

G. J.

Canberra
July 1962

SYMBOLS AND ABBREVIATIONS

Where necessary, long vowels are marked with a macron (e.g. *ā*), and short vowels with a curl (*ă*). Open *e* and *o* are marked with a hook (*ę*, *ǫ*), close *e* and *o* with a dot (*ẹ*, *ọ*). In citations of OE forms, a dot placed above *c*, *g*, *cg* and *sc* (i.e. *ċ*, *ġ*, *ċġ*, *sċ*) indicates palatal quality. The symbol [χ] indicates the voiceless velar spirant (as in Scots *loch*), [ʒ] the corresponding voiced spirant; [š] indicates the voiceless sound (as in ME *schall*), [ž] the corresponding voiced sound. The classes of strong verbs are given Roman numerals (I-VII), those of the weak verbs Arabic (1-3).

The following are the main abbreviations:

acc.	accusative	N	Northern
adj.	adjective	n.	noun
adv.	adverb	nom.	nominative
AN	Anglo-Norman	num.	numeral
Angl.	Anglian	nWS	non West Saxon
art.	article	obl.	oblique
C	Chaucer	OE	Old English
CF	Central French	OF	Old French
cpv.	comparative	ON	Old Norse
dat.	dative	pers.	person
dem.	demonstrative	pl.	plural
E	Eastern	poss.	possessive
EM	East Midland	p.p.	preterite participle
eME	early Middle English	pres.	present
fem.	feminine	pret.	preterite
gen.	genitive	pron.	pronoun
Gmc	Germanic	ptc.	participle
imp.	imperative	refl.	reflexive
indef.	indefinite	rel.	relative
ind(ic).	indicative	S	Southern
inf.	infinitive	sg.	singular
Kt.	Kentish	sjv.	subjunctive
Lat.	Latin	spv.	superlative
lME	late ME	Std(E)	Standard English
lOE	late OE	SW	South Western
lWS	late West Saxon	v.	verb
M	Midland	VL	Vulgar Latin
masc.	masculine	W	Western
Mcn	Mercian	WGmc	West Germanic
ME	Middle English	WM	West Midland
ModE	Modern English	WS	West Saxon

I INTRODUCTION

§1 'Middle English' is the name given to the type of English used from about 1100 to about 1500.

It is distinguished from the preceding type, 'Old English' (also called 'Anglo-Saxon'), by the gradual cessation from written use of the Late Old English (i.e. West Saxon) standard language. This fell into abeyance after the Norman Conquest, when French (i.e. Anglo-Norman) became the language of the court, the royal offices, the law courts, the schools, and indeed of educated people generally, while English was employed only in documents of a more practical sort, especially works of religious instruction. English did not re-establish itself as the language of the educated until the 13th and 14th centuries.

Middle English is distinguished from the succeeding type, 'Modern English', by the spread throughout England—but not Scotland—of the London dialect as a standard language.

Middle English is not a uniform language. Texts from the 11th and 12th centuries still have many forms proper to the lOE standard language, mixed with spellings reflecting changes which had occurred in the meantime. Later, individual scribes tried to represent their own dialects, using as a basis the sound-values of the letters in French or Latin orthography; but fairly well established local spelling systems did not develop until the second half of the 14th century, and these too largely disappeared after 1450 in favour of London forms, although even in the London standard language a number of alternative forms were still being used at the close of the 15th century.

§2 Our knowledge of the regional distribution of the forms of Middle English is based on the following:

1. *Spellings*, in documents whose provenance can be established. These are charters particularly, although those written in English only appear relatively late, and 15th century charters, even in other parts of the country, already exhibit many forms from the language of the royal offices in London. Spellings in MSS of other classes of writing whose place of origin is known have also to be considered, when the copies come from much the

same area. A ME scribe usually copied his texts in his own dialect, but in many instances this was not done thoroughly, so
that forms from the exemplar were sometimes taken over unaltered.

2. *Rimes*, in poems whose author's place of origin can be
identified. It has to be noted, however, that to find rimes more
easily poets occasionally used some which were not proper to
their own dialects. Again, when poems were copied or revised,
rimes which did not conform to the dialect of the copyist or
reviser were often modified.

3. *Place-names*, especially older forms of them.

4. *Forms reconstructed* from those of the dialects of Modern
English.

§3   The dialects of Middle English to some extent reproduce
features already recognised in Old English; to some extent, also,
the development of the language in Middle English differs from
place to place.

In the South the dialect of Kent is clearly distinct from others
as it was in Old English, and likewise the South Western dialects derived from West Saxon. The dialect of Essex and its
environs is first known to us in Middle English. That of London
we know from the 12th century, but it is not extensively docu-
mented until the second half of the 14th (e.g. in Chaucer's works
and numerous charters); at the outset it exhibits Southern characteristics, but later adopts to an increasing extent forms first
attested in the East Midlands (Lincolnshire and nearby areas).

In the Anglian region in Middle English, speech north and
south of the Humber is distinguished by fundamental differences.

From the southern area, the Midlands, we have from both
the East (Lincolnshire, Norfolk) and the West numerous documents of known origin, so that the dialectal characteristics can
be quite well established. The East and the West are clearly
distinct, and the latter has some features in common with the
South West.

The dialects of the districts north of the Humber, those of
Northern English, are known to us only from a relatively later
period (the end of the 13th century and beginning of the 14th),
but then from quite plentiful evidence; here too, the West and
the East differ, and in addition, Scots as it appears in 15th cen-

tury literary texts differs from the rest of Northern English.

§4 The ME dialects differ not only in forms (sounds, inflexions, and partly syntax) but also in vocabulary. Notably, the Southern dialects have many more French loanwords than those of the Midlands and North, except the Scots literary language; and the dialects of the East Midlands and the North have a much greater Norse element than the others.

§5 ME spelling is derived partly from OE methods and partly from French and Latin orthography; some innovations also appear.

A Old English

The OE letters þ and ʒ remain throughout ME. About 1400 *th* becomes common beside þ, without any obvious difference in usage; this is due particularly to the fact that in the hand of the period, þ had become similar to *y*, if not identical with it. Up to the end of the 13th century, ð still appears here and there, beside þ.

As the symbol of the voiced guttural stop, *g* replaces ʒ. The latter[1] then indicates only the voiced spirants (palatal or velar); but is later used also for the corresponding voiceless spirants. Some scribes use ʒh instead of plain ʒ. About 1300, the voiced palatal spirant is spelt *y* as well as ʒ, and some scribes also use *g*.

The runic letter Ƿ (wynn) is still used quite generally in the 12th century and extensively up to the middle of the 13th, but is less frequent after that, being replaced by *w*.

As a result of sound-changes, æ and *ea* are replaced by *a* or *e* gradually after the 12th century, generally after 1250. In MSS of the 12th century and the first half of the 13th, *ea* appears as a a spelling for [ę̄], even when this does not derive from OE *ea*, and in the 14th century it is found as a spelling for [ę̄] in Anglo-Norman MSS, and then in English as well, first in French words.

Until the 15th century *eo* is retained as the symbol for the sound [ö] derived from *eo* (§10) in the areas where this sound remains; it is also used occasionally (e.g. in *people*) to denote the [ö] from French *ué*.

---

[1] The reader is asked to note that whereas the phonetic symbol [ʒ] is used in this book to denote the voiced velar spirant, the letter ʒ can represent, in ME forms, any of the sounds mentioned in this paragraph. This letter is derived from the OE form (taken over from Irish handwriting) of *g*.

B French

French spelling is responsible for the use of *u* to indicate the sound [ü]; the OE spelling, *y*, is dropped, and—apart from representing the voiced palatal spirant (see A above)—*y* is used interchangeably with *i*. Occasionally, especially in 15th century MSS, [ü] is spelt *ui* or *uy*.

The sound [ö] is sometimes spelt *ue*, but also *o* and *u*.

In the second half of the 13th century [u] is spelt *o* rather than *u*, as CF *o* often corresponds to AN *u*; being more legible, *o* establishes itself as a spelling of [u], especially next to *n*, *m*, *v* (written *u*) and *w*. After 1300 [ū] is regularly spelt *ou*, as in French.

Except in a few MSS, *ie* is not a regular spelling for [ẹ̄] until the 15th century; it appears first in French words.

As in French (but contrary to OE custom) *c* is used for the sound [k] only before *a*, *o* and *u*; before *e* and *i* it denotes [s].

The following are also French spellings: *g* for the voiced guttural stop (see A above); *i*, *j*, *gg* or *dg* for [dž]; *qu* instead of OE *cw*; *ch* for [tš]; *z* for the voiced sibilant (the OE spelling, which also survives into ME, was *s*, as for the voiceless sound); and *v*, often spelt *u*, for the voiced labiodental spirant (spelt *f* in OE, along with the voiceless sound).

C Innovations

New methods of representing sounds are *gh* for the voiceless velar or palatal spirant (also spelt ȝ, in the North *ch*, and in some MSS, especially early ones, still *h* as in OE), and *sch* (later also *sh*) instead of OE *sc* for [š].

From the 13th century *hw* is spelt *wh*, in the North *quh* or *qu*; the latter also appears in the East Midlands (Norfolk).

In some MSS long vowels, except [ū], are indicated by doubling (*aa*, *ee*, rarely *ii*), and short vowels sometimes by doubling the following consonant. After final *-e* became silent (§ 27), an *e* after a single consonant is frequently used to indicate the length of the vowel of the preceding syllable; but meaningless instances of final *-e* also occur, especially in 15th century MSS.

Note 1 Consistent spelling is maintained in the MS of the *Orrmulum*, a paraphrase of the Gospels with commentary, by the Augustinian canon Orrm (or Orrmin), written about 1200 in the East Midlands. As a rule

Orrm indicates short vowels by doubling the following consonant; he also takes pains to use only one letter for each sound in order to distinguish them.

Note 2   AN scribes, whose command of English was evidently incomplete, often confuse letters unfamiliar to them, such as þ, ȝ and ƿ. They also confuse similar letters, such as v and ƿ, ȝ and z; and insert h incorrectly, as in *th* for *ht*, and so on. Some mistakes of this sort are still found in 14th century MSS, and even later.

Note 3   In the 15th century particularly, *j*, which was very similar to the capital *I*, is occasionally written for *i*, whether by itself (as in the pronoun *I*) or in the prefix *i-* (OE *ȝe-*).

Note 4   The abbreviations customary in French and Latin MSS of the period are also used by ME scribes.

Note 5   As [ai] had become [ā] in parts of Northern England and Scotland from the middle of the 14th century, in these districts *i* is used as a mark of length not only after *a* but also after *o* and *u*, as in *oi* for [ǭ] and [ọ̄], and *ui* for [ū]; spellings of *ei* for *ē*, *ai* for *ā*, and conversely *a* for *ai* also occur in some (perhaps Eastern) 15th century texts.

II PHONOLOGY

Part 1 Vowels

Vowels of Stressed Syllables

Summary

§6 The following vowels occur in stressed syllables in Middle English:

A Short Vowels

[a] spelt *a*, and in the 12th century also *æ* and *ea*
— from OE *æ* (§11.1), *a* (§11.7), *ea* (§10), shortened *ǣ* (§9) and *ā* (§9); ON *a* (§17); and OF *a* (§§21 and 22A)

[e] spelt *e*, and in the 12th century also *ea*
— from OE *e* (§11.7 and §10, n. 1 and n. 2), *ea* (lOE *e* after palatal consonants, §10, n. 1 and n. 5, or as the result of smoothing, §10, n. 1 and n. 4), *eo* (by way of [ö], §10), shortened *ēa*, *ǣ* and *ē* (§9), *y* (in Kent and the South East, §11.5), and *i* (in special instances, §11, n. 16); ON *e* (§17); and OF *e* (§§21 and 22A)

[i] spelt *i* or *y*
— from OE *i* (§11.7), *y* (§11.5), shortened *ī* (§9) and *ē* and *ēo* (§9, n.), ON *i* (§17); and OF *i* (§§21 and 22A) and [ü] in special instances (§22, n. 2)

[o] spelt *o*
— from OE *o* (§11.7), *a* or *o* before nasals (§11.3), shortened *ō* (§9) and *ā* (§9, n., Southern); ON *o* (§17); and OF *o* (§§21 and 22A)

[u] spelt *u* or *o*, sometimes *ou*
— from OE *u* (§11.7), shortened *ū* (§9) and *ō* (§9, n.), *y* after labial (§11.5); ON *u* (§17); AN *u* (§§21 and 22A, 22B.3, 4); and OF [ü] (short, cf. §21 and §23.2a), and *ui* (§23, n. 5)

[ö] spelt *eo*
— from OE *eo* (unrounded to [e] early in ME, §10)

[ü] spelt *u*
— from OE *y* (only in the West, later *i* or *u*, §11.5)

B Long Vowels

ā] spelt *a* or *aa*, in the North also *ai* (§5, n.5)
—from OE *ā* (eME and Northern, §11.4), *a* before lengthening groups (Northern, §§8 and 11.4), *a*, *æ* and *ea* in open syllables (§12A), and *ǣ* (in East Saxon, §11.2); ON *ā* (Northern, §§17 and 11.4); OF *a* (long, cf. §§21 and 22A); and ME *ai* (Northern, §13, n. 1) and *au* before labials and [š] and [ž] (§§22, n. 2 and 22B.1)

ę̄] spelt *e*, *ee*, and *ea* (§5A)
—from OE *ǣ* (§11.2), *ēa* (§§10 and 11.2), and *e* in open syllables (§12A); ON *ei* before *k* (§18); OF *e* (long, cf. §§21 and 22A), and *ai* and *ei* before dentals (§22B.5); and ME [ęu] before labials (§23.8)

ẹ̄] spelt *e* or *ee*, later also *ie* (cf. §5B)
—from OE *ē* (§11.7), *ēo* (by way of [ō̤], §10); *ȳ* (Kentish and South Eastern, §11.5), *e* and *eo* before lengthening groups (§8), and *i* in open syllables (§12B); ON *ē* (§17); OF *é* from Latin *a* in open syllables (§22A), *ié* (§22B.6), and *ué* (by way of [ō̤], §23.3); and ME [ęu] before labials (§22, n. 2)

ī] spelt *i* or *y*, occasionally *ii*
—from OE *ī* (§11.7), *ȳ* (§11.5), *i* or *y* before lengthening groups (§8), *i* before [χ'] (§13C.8) and *ē* before [χ'] (§13C.7), *ē* + ʒ, *ĭ* + ʒ, *ў̆* + ʒ (§13A.4, 5, 6, 7); ON *ī* and *ȳ* (§17); OF *i* (long, cf. §§21 and 22A); and ME *iu* before labials and [š] and [ž] (§22, n. 2)

ǭ] spelt *o* or *oo*
—from OE and ON *ā* (Southern, §11.4), OE *o* in open syllables (§12A); OF *o* (long, cf. §§21 and 22A); and ME *ou* before labials (§22, n. 2) and *oi* (Northern, §23, n. 5)

ọ̄] spelt *o* or *oo*
—from OE *ō* (§11.7), *ā* after *w* and in weakly stressed syllables (§11, n. 11), and *o* before lengthening groups (§8); ON *ō* (§17); and OF *o* (long, cf. §21) next to labials (§22A)

ū] spelt *u*, *ou* or *ow*
—from OE *ū* (§11.7), *u* before lengthening groups (§8), *ōw* and *ōʒ* (§13B.4), *ŭʒ* (§13B.5), *ō* before [χ] (§13C.3), *ŭ* before [χ] (§13C.4, 5); ON *ū* (§17); AN *u* (long, cf. §§21, 22A and 22B.3, 4); and OF [ü] (long, cf. §21—in a limited area, §23, n. 2)

ō̤] spelt *eo*, *ue*, *u* or *o*; later [ẹ̄], §10
—from OE *ēo* (§10), and OF *ué* (§23.3)

ǖ] spelt *u* or *ui*
—from OE *ȳ* (Southern and Western, §11.5), *ō* (Northern, §11.6); OF [ü] (long, cf. §§21 and 23.2*b*), [üi] (§23.6), later often [iu] (§23.2*b*)

C Diphthongs

[ai] spelt *ai*, *ei*, *ay* and *ey*
— from OE *æӡ*, *eӡ* and *ǣӡ* (§13A.1,2,3), *ў̆ӡ* (Kentish and Sout
Eastern, §13A.7); ON *ei* and *ey* (§18); OF *ai*, AN *ei* (§22B.5), *a* an
e before [l′] and [n′] (§22B.7); and ME *a* before [ndž], [ntš] and [š
(§13D.3)

[ei] spelt *ei* or *ey*; later [ai] or [ī]
— from OE *ēӡ* (§13A.4), *ē* before [χ′] (§13C.7), *ў̆ӡ* (Kentish, §13A.7)
and ME *e* before [š] (§13D.3)

[oi] spelt *oi* or *oy*
— from OF *oi* (§23.4), and CF *oi* (AN *ei*, §22, n. 5)

[ui] spelt *ui* or *oi*
— from AN *ui* (§23.5), and *u* before [l′] and [n′] (§22B.7)

[üi] spelt *ui* or *u*; later coalesced with OF [ü]
— from OF *üi* (§23.6)

[au] spelt *au* or *aw*
— from OE *aw* and *aӡ* (§13B.1), *āw* and *āӡ* (Northern, §13B.2
and *a* before [χ] (§13C.1); ON *a* (§18); OF *au* (§22A); AN *au* befor
nasals (§22B.1); and ME *ou* (§13, n. 7 and n. 11)

[ǫu] spelt *ou* or *ow*
— from OE *ow* and *oӡ* (§13B.3), *āw* and *āӡ* (Southern, §13B.2
and *o* before [χ] (§13C.2); ON *au* and *ou* (§18); and OF *ou* (§22A

[ọu] spelt *ou* or *ow*; later [ū] or [ǫu] south of the Humber
— from OE *ōw* and *ōӡ* (§13B.4), and *ō* before [χ] (§13C.3)

[ẹu] spelt *eu* or *ew*
— from OE *ǣw*, *ēaw* and *ēow* (§13B.6,7); and OF *eau* (§23.8)

[ẹu], [iu] spelt *eu*, *ew*, *iu*, *iw* or *u*
— from OE *ēow* (§13B.8) and *īw* (§13B.9); and OF *ieu* (§23.7) an
ü (§23.2*b*)

[ŭō] spelt *uo* or *wo*
— from ME *ō* after *b* and *g* (§13D.1), and initially (§13D.2)

[ĭē] spelt *ye*
— from ME *ē* initially (§13D.2)

Historical Development

native element

§7   In OE the following vowels occurred in stressed syllables
(*a*) short monophthongs: *a*, *æ*, *e*, *i*, *o*, *u*, and *y* [ü];
(*b*) long monophthongs: *ā*, *ǣ*, *ē*, *ī*, *ō*, *ū*, and *ȳ* [ǖ];

(c) short diphthongs: *ea, eo, io* (only in Northumbrian at the end of the OE period), and *ie* (only in West Saxon, and replaced by *y* or *i* at the end of the period);

(d) long diphthongs: *ēa, ēo, īo* (only in Kentish at the end of the period), and *īe* (only in West Saxon, and replaced by *ȳ* or *ī* at the end of the period).

§8 Lengthening Before Certain Consonant Groups

Short vowels, both monophthongs and diphthongs, had already been lengthened in the 8th century or the first half of the 9th before a liquid or nasal consonant followed by a homorganic voiced stop (*ld, mb, nd, ng, rd, rn*) and before *r* followed by a homorganic voiced spirant (*rs, rð, rl*). The results were the corresponding long vowels and diphthongs (that is, *ā, ǣ, ē, ī, ō, ū, ȳ, ēa, ēo* or *īo*, and *īe* or *ȳ* from *a, æ, e, i, o, u, y, ea, eo* or *io*, and *ie* or *y* respectively), which then had the same development as the old long sounds (§§10 and 11).

Lengthening did not take place, however, (1) when another consonant followed one of the groups listed, so that we have *cĭld* sg., *cĭldru* pl.; *lāmb* or *lōmb* sg., *lămbru* or *lŏmbru* pl.; *sēndan* inf., *sĕnd(d)e* pret.; and the short vowel in these forms sometimes caused the lengthening in other forms to be levelled out; (2) in words with reduced sentence stress, such as *ŭnder, ănd, wŏlde* etc.

During the ME period these long sounds were shortened again in Kentish, and in other dialects before *rd, ng* and *nd*; this explains such forms in Modern Standard English as *land*, compared with Southern ME *lǭnd* (cf. §11.4), *among, long*, etc. In Northern and Eastern dialects lengthening before final *-nd* and *-rd* probably never occurred at all, as final *-d* had been unvoiced.

§9 Shortening of Long Vowels

In the 10th century, and later in similar conditions, long vowels were shortened:

1. Before groups of two consonants, except those listed in §8 as causing lengthening and those in which both consonants (e.g. *st, sm*) had been transferred to the second syllable. Thus in lOE there were short vowels in *leoht, liht* 'light', *softe* 'soft', *feoll* 'fell', the syncopated preterites *cepte* and *bledde* (from *cēpan* and *blēdan*), compounds such as *wisdom* and *wifman*, and syn-

B

copated inflexions such as *halǵes* (gen. of *hāliǵ*). On the other
hand, long vowels remained in *frēond* 'friend', *fēond* 'enemy',
hērde or *hȳrde* (pret. of *hēran* 'to hear'), *hēold* 'held', *blōsma*
'blossom', and in inflected forms such as *mǣsta* 'greatest' and
gāstes (gen. of *gast* 'spirit'), from which, indeed, the long vowel
was often transferred to the uninflected shortened forms.

2. In antepenultimate syllables, where these still existed, as
in *hĕafodu* (pl. of *hēafod* 'head'), *hăliǵdæǵ* 'holyday', *sŭþerne*
'southern', etc.

3. In some words which often had reduced sentence stress,
such as *ăn* 'one' (as indefinite article), *lăt* and *lĕt* 'let' (from
OE *lǣtan*, *lētan*).

Note The results were the corresponding short vowels, which then
had the same development in ME as the old short sounds (§§10, 11
and 13C).

The first set of shortenings preceded the changes of OE *æ* to *a*, OE *ā*
to Southern *ǭ*, and OE *ō* to Northern [ǖ] described in §11.1, 4, 6, and
those before [χt] listed in §13C. Thus ME has *a* for WS *ǣ* from WGmc *ā*
beside *e* (from *ē* in the other OE dialects), as in *lat* beside *let* and *Strat-*
beside *Stret-* in the first element of placenames, and *a* for OE *ā* from
Gmc *ai*, as in *halidai*.

As shortened and unshortened forms of the same word often existed
side by side (e.g. in the first element of compounds compared with un-
compounded words, or in different inflexions) there still existed forms
with a long vowel which were capable of being shortened. Accordingly,
there is a later set of shortenings in which—because of the changes
described in §11 which had occurred meanwhile—OE *ǣ* was shortened
to *e*, OE *ā* in the South to *o*, OE *ē* to *i*, and OE *ō* to *u* (in the North by
way of [ü], cf. §11.6). Thus ME has *lefdi* beside *lafdi* 'lady' (OE *hlǣfdiǵe*),
left beside *laft* 'left', *lest* beside *last* 'last', *holiday* beside *haliday*, *fil* beside
fel 'fell' (OE *fēoll*), *sick* beside *seknesse* 'sickness', and in the South often
gud beside *good* 'good'.

§10 Monophthongisation of OE Diphthongs

All the OE diphthongs had become monophthongs by the
11th century at the latest; in Kent alone the long diphthongs
ēa and *īo* survived (see §11, n. 20; *īo* had taken the place of the
ēo of other dialects).

Accordingly, *ĕa* became *æ* (coalescing with OE *æ*, see §11);
ēa became *ǣ* (coalescing with OE *ǣ*, see §11); *ĕo* and *ēo* became
[ö] and [ȫ], still usually spelt *eo*. This sound [ö] was unrounded
to *e* and *ē* in the 12th century, and then spelt *e* or *ee*, in all
districts (including Kent) except the West and South, where

the unrounding did not take place until later—in the 14th century at the latest for the long sound, earlier for the short—and in these areas *eo*-spellings remained here and there until the 15th century. The spelling was sometimes *ue, o* or *u* instead of *eo* (see §23.3).

Note 1 Observe that:

1. *ea* as a result of breaking is common to all OE dialects only before *rr* and *r* plus consonant; before *ll* and *l* plus consonant, Anglian has *a* for WS and Kentish *ea*, hence Angl. *ald* beside *eald*, Angl. *half* beside *healf*. Even before *rd* and *rn, rm* OE has sporadic *a*, as in *arm* beside *earm*. The distinction is apparent in ME only when there is lengthening before consonant groups (§8), and not when the short vowels remain, because *æ* (from *ea*) and *a* later coalesced in *a* (§11.1). The scope of *ea* before *ll* and *l* plus consonant comprised the old West Saxon area, southern Essex and Kent, but northerly forms derived from OE *a* became more common in the South, in London especially, in the course of the ME period.

2. As a result of *i*-mutation, OE *ĕa* had become *ĭe*, later *ў* in West Saxon, *ĕ* in Anglian and Kentish. In West Saxon *ĭo* had also become *ĭe*, later *ў*, by *i*-mutation; Anglian and Kentish retained *ĭo* and *ĕo*. Again by *i*-mutation, *a* (instead of *ea*) before *ll, l* plus consonant, *rr* and *r* plus consonant had become in some places *æ*, in others *e*. The forms in ME attest developments corresponding to the OE dialectal differences, thus: ME *elder, alder, ulder* for OE *eldra, ældra, yldra*; 'older'; ME *heere(n), hure(n)* for OE *hēran, hўran* 'to hear'; ME *herde, hurde* for OE *hiorde, heorde, hierde, hyrde* 'shepherd'; ME *stere(n), sture(n)* for OE *stēoran, stīoran, stīeran, stȳran* 'to steer'.

3. The group *weor-*, produced by breaking or back mutation, had become *wor-* or *wur-* generally at the end of the OE period; only when *-c* followed had *eo* sometimes remained or become *e* by Anglian smoothing: thus OE *weorc, werc* beside *worc, wurc*. We cannot decide whether the ME spelling *o* represents [o] or [u], because [u] was often spelt *o*, particularly next to *w*, see §5B. ME *werk* reproduces OE *werc* with Anglian smoothing, or is influenced by ON (O Dan *Värk*, O Icel *Verk*).

WS *wier-, wyr-* (with *i*-mutation of *io* or *u*) had become *wur-* in the South in lOE. In the North the corresponding form is *wir-*, unrounded from OE *wyr-*, which is itself the result of the *i*-mutation of OE *wur-*, since *i* between *w* and *r* had already become *u* in Northumbrian early in OE. Thus ME has *wurse, worse* beside Northern *wirse* from OE *wiersa, wyrsa* 'worse'; *wurþe* beside Northern *wirþe* from OE *wyrþe* 'worthy'; and *wurche, worche* beside *wirk* from OE *wyrċan* 'to work'.

ME *werld*, beside *world, wurld* 'world', and *werse* 'worse' have been influenced by Norse.

4. Before *h* [χ] almost all diphthongs had been smoothed to monophthongs already in OE, i.e. *ea* had become *æ* in Anglian, *e* in WS and Kentish (and sporadically in Anglian too, before *ht*); *ēa* had become *ē*

generally; *ĕo*, *ĭo* before *ht*, and *ĭe* invariably had become *ĭ*, save that *ĕo* had become *ĕ* before a back vowel. On later developments, see §13C.

5. In OE there are two sets of diphthongs produced by palatal consonants (*ġ* and *ċ*) before vowels, and we have to distinguish:

(A) an older stratum, in which Prim.OE *æ* became at first *ea* and then *e*, or by contemporaneous *i*-mutation *ie*, later *i*; and Prim.OE *e* became first *ie*, later *i*. This diphthongisation was predominantly West Saxon; the other dialects kept *æ* (which became *e* by *i*-mutation) and *e*. Forms to be explained by these changes also occur in ME outside the WS area proper. We thus have Southern *shell* beside *shall* from OE *sceal* 'shall'; *shill* beside *shell* 'shell'; and, more widely spread, *ʒiue(n)* beside *ʒeue(n)* from OE *ġiefan*, *ġifan*, *ġefan* 'to give'; further, *-chester* (Latin *castra*) not only in the South but also in the Midlands and North in placenames such as *Chester-le-Street* (Durham), *Manchester*, *Chester*, *Chesterfield* (Derbyshire), *Lanchester* (Durham), *Irchester* (S.E. Northants), *Grantchester* (near Cambridge) and *Colchester* (Essex), but also *-caster*, probably because of sound-substitution by the Norse settlers, in *Lancaster* (Lancashire), *Doncaster* (Yorkshire), *Casterton* (Rutland) and *Castor* (near Peterborough). The OE diphthongisation of back vowels after *ġ* (Gmc *j*), as in OE *ġeong* beside *ġung* 'young' and *ġeāra* 'yore', leaves no traces in ME, where the forms are *ʒung*, *ʒong* and (Southern) *ʒǭre* (cf. §11.4). The ME form *ʒing*, frequent in rimes in popular verse, may derive from the Old Northumbrian form *ġing* (which is the result of palatal influence) or from the comparative (WS *ġingra*).

(B) a younger stratum, in which back vowels were diphthongised after OE *sċ*, as in OE *sċeamu*, *sċeomu* 'shame'. The results here were probably rising diphthongs, which generally reverted to simple back vowels in ME. In ME *silf* (beside *self*) can be seen the lWS and Kentish change of *e* to *y* or *i* in the group *sel*. Similarly, ME *siggen* beside *seggen* 'to say' is to be explained by the change of *e* to *i* before OE *ċġ*.

Note 2 The monophthongisation of *ĕa* took place about 1000. A few spellings of *æ* for *ea* and conversely *ea* for *æ* already appear in some MSS of the end of the 10th century, and in the 11th they become commoner.

The monophthongisation of *ĕo* cannot be dated, because the spelling *eo* continued to be used until the [ö] sound was unrounded. In the first two-thirds of his work Orrm wrote *eo*, but the *-o* has been erased and only restored by a reviser. Apparently, in Orrm's time the rounding had gradually been dropped in his district.

§11   Qualitative Changes of the OE Vowels

1.   OE *æ*

OE *æ* (including *æ* from *ea*, §10) became *a*: hence ME *appel* 'apple' (OE *æppel*), ME *bak* 'back' (OE *bæċ*), ME *sat* 'sat' (OE *sæt*), ME *ale* 'ale' (OE *ealu*), and ME *arm* 'arm' (OE *earm*).

Note 1 From the 13th century the spelling *a* became general. In MSS of the 12th and early 13th centuries the traditional spelling *æ* or *ea* is still found, often used erroneously without regard to the OE forms.

Note 2 In those areas (i.e. Kent and the West Midlands) where OE had *e* instead of *æ*, *e* at first remained in ME, as in *eppel*, *blek*, *bek* etc., but *a* became predominant in the West Midlands in the 13th century and in Kent in the 14th. In these areas OE *ea* is also *a*, as in *arm*, *hard*, *all* etc.

Note 3 The forms *wes* beside *was*, *hedde* beside *hadde* are not dialectal; they are due rather to the frequent occurrence of these words in positions with secondary stress in the sentence. Norse influence is the probable reason for *gress* beside *grass*, French for *messe* beside *masse*.

Note 4 As a result of the OE change after palatal consonants (see §10, n. 1, para. 5), *e* appears for OE *ea* after ME *ch*, *ȝ* and *sch* in the far North, the West Midlands and the South.

2. OE *ǣ*

OE *ǣ* (including *ǣ* from *ēa*, §10) became ME [ẹ̄], spelt *e* or *ee*, except in the East Saxon area, where it became *ā* although *ēa* became [ẹ̄]. In OE, WGmc *ā* had given *ǣ* only in West Saxon and East Anglian, elsewhere becoming *ē*; so that the ME forms vary as follows: West Saxon and East Anglian *strẹ̄t*, East Saxon *strāt*, Kentish and Anglian *strẹ̄t*; similarly *drẹ̄de(n)*, *drāde(n)*, *drẹ̄de(n)* 'to dread'; for OE *ǣ* from WGmc *ai* with *i*-mutation, however, we have East Saxon *lāren*, elsewhere *lẹ̄re(n)* ' to teach'; East Saxon *dāl*, elsewhere *dẹ̄l* 'part'; but general ME *dẹ̄f* (OE *dēaf*) 'deaf'.

Note 5 The area of ME *ā* for OE *ǣ*, briefly called 'East Saxon' above, includes Essex, Hertfordshire, Bedfordshire, and probably also parts of Cambridge and Middlesex; but although London is nearby, the upper class London dialect of Chaucer has no instances of *ā*.

Note 6 The boundary between OE *ǣ* and *ē* for WGmc *ā* is most clearly discernible in place-names whose first element is *strǣt* or *strēt* shortened, because the shortening produced *a* in the area with *ǣ*, against *e* in the area with *ē*, as in *Stratford* and *Stretford*. On this basis it runs from the Wash through Cambridgeshire towards Northants and Warwick and along the old northern limit of the diocese of Worcester to the Severn. Kent, however, belongs to the area with *ē*.

Note 7 Rimes of *ẹ̄* and *ę̄* are avoided only by poets who rime strictly, and in popular poetry are common, especially before dentals, where *ę̄* seems to have had a closer pronunciation in some districts, particularly in the North.

Note 8 WGmc *ā* remained in Old Norse, so that in ME we also have *ī* instead of *ẹ̄* in Norse loanwords in Northern English (see §17 and section 4 below).

3. OE *a* OR *o* BEFORE NASALS

OE *a* or *o* before nasals, except when lengthened before consonant groups (§8), is *a* in ME except in the West Midlands,
where it is *o*: hence ME *man*, WM *mon* 'man'; ME *name*, WM
nome (with lengthening in an open syllable, §12).

Note 9 In unstressed words, such as *on* 'an', *o* is general in the rest
of England as well. In *hwonne* 'when' and *ponne* 'then' the *o*-forms were
later ousted by forms with *-a-* and *-e-*. *Moni* is widespread, particularly
in Scotland where it is the only form in use; and similarly *oni* in place of
ani, *eni* (OE *æniġ* with shortening, §9.2). This form *oni* is the result of
analogy with *moni*, or with *ǫn* 'one'.

4. OE *ā*

OE *ā* was rounded to *ǫ*, spelt *o* or *oo*, between the 11th century and the 12th, south of a line running west from the Humber. (The change begins in the south and works northward.
North of this line, *ā* remained. Thus we have S *bon*, *boon*, N *ban*,
bain (§5, n. 5) from OE *bān* 'bone'; S *grope*(*n*), N *grape* 'to grip';
S *hond*, *hoond*, N *hand* (with lengthening before *nd*, §8); S *oolo*
beside WS and Kentish *ęęld* (§§8 and 10, n. 1, para. 1), N *āld* 'old'.

Note 10 Spellings with *o* for *ā* first crop up in MSS in the early 12th
century. In Southern MSS they become common in the course of that
century, and general in the 13th. In the Midlands variation in spelling
lasts longer, and in the North Midlands it is still not fixed in the 14th
century. The modern division among the dialects is probably arrived at
in the 15th century. Popular verse, probably from border areas, rimes
words containing OE *ā* with *ō* or *ā* at need.
Note 11 The later development of *ǫ* (OE *ō*) differs from that of *ǫ*
in both ME and ModE, but only the more careful ME poets avoid
riming the two sounds.

OE *o* before nasals (section 3 above) was lengthened to *ǫ* before consonant groups (§8) in the West Midlands.

After *hw-*, *w* preceded by a consonant, and in weakly stressed syllables
ǫ became *ǭ*, as in *who* 'who', *two* 'two' (ModE [tū]), and in the suffix
-hood (OE *-hād*).

5. OE *ȳ*

OE *ȳ* [ǖ] had become *ē* in Kent about 900. The evidence of
ME documents indicates that this change also occurred in Essex
in parts of Suffolk and Hertfordshire, in Sussex (where it is
found in place-names beside *i-* and *ü-*forms), and probably in
Middlesex and southern Cambridgeshire too.

North of this region and east of a line which runs southwards down the Pennine chain to London, and also in Westmorland and Cumberland and in a small area in the west (Devonshire and Dorset), *ў* was unrounded to *ĭ* in the 10th or 11th century.

Only in the South West (except Dorset and Devon) and the West Midlands (including Lancashire), then, was the rounded [ü] retained, and spelt *u*, as in French, §5B.

The variants in ME are thus: *kisse(n)*, *kesse(n)*, *cusse(n)* 'to kiss' from OE *cyssan*; *sinne*, *senne*, *sunne* 'sin' from OE *synn*; *fĭr*, *fĕr*, *fŭr* 'fire' from OE *fŷr*.

Note 12 The first instance of *e* for *y* is in the Kentish Glosses (c. 900). Unrounding to *i* is first discernible in spellings of *i* instead of *y* in Northumbrian texts from the end of the OE period, although these are rare. The retention of the rounded sound is not definitely indicated until the introduction of the spelling *u*.

Note 13 lWS *ŷ* for older *īe* likewise became [ü] in ME, spelt *u*, as in SW *ulder* 'older', *hure(n)* 'to hear', *hurde* 'shepherd' and *sture(n)* 'to steer'. Cf. §10, n. 1, para. 2.

Note 14 lWS *y* from *i*, near labials and before *r*, is also [ü] in ME, spelt *u*, as in *schup* 'ship', *muchel* (OE *mićel*, *myćel*) 'much', *furst* 'period of time', *churche* 'church'.

Note 15 Next to a palatal, *i* for OE *y* appears even in the West, as a result of the OE unrounding in this position; hence ME *king* (OE *cyning*, *cining*) 'king'.

The rounded Western sound remained into the 15th century, until superseded by *i*. But after labials, next to [š] and [tš], and before *r*, it became [u], as is clearly indicated by occasional spellings with *o*, hence *muchel*, *muche*, *moche* 'much', *burden* 'burden', *churche* 'church', and *shutte(n)* 'to shut'.

6. OE *ō*

OE *ō*, about the 14th century, north of a line running west from the Humber, became an [ü] sound, more and more commonly spelt *u* or *ui*, which rimes with French [ü] (§23.2B): thus *gude* and *guid* instead of *good* 'good', *blud* and *bluid* instead of *blood* 'blood', and so on. Elsewhere *ō* remained as a close [ọ].

7. OE *a*, *ĕ*, *ĭ*, *o*, *ŭ*

OE *a*, *ē* (as a close sound), *ī* and *ū* remained unaltered in ME. The short vowels *e*, *i*, *o* and *u* also remained, but seem to have had a closer pronunciation in OE than in the 12th century,

because the results of the lOE lengthening before consonant
groups (§8) differ from those of the ME lengthening in open
syllables (§12).

Note 16   Between *ʒ* or *g* and a dental, between *r* and a dental, and
before a supported nasal *e* became *i* in various parts of England, hence
togidere beside *togedere* 'together', *yis* beside *yes*, *brinne(n)* beside *bren-
ne(n)* 'to burn' (ON *brenna*), *inglisch* 'English', *stringth* beside *strength*
'strength', *singen* beside *sengen* 'to singe', and the Southern ending of
the pres.ptc. *-inde* beside Midland *-ende*.

(Conversely, *e* appears for *i* in numerous MSS, particularly after *w* as
in *sweft* beside *swift*, before *l* as in *stelle* beside *stille*, and in the 15th
century also before *r* as in *Ser* for *Sir*, *berd* for *bird*, and *merrour* beside
mirrour 'mirror'.)

A corresponding change of *o* to *u* seems to have occurred next to
labials, as in *brusten* beside *brosten* (from ON, alongside *borsten* from OE)
and perhaps also in *murp*, *murper*, *murder* 'murder', although in this
word the influence of AN *murdrer* (OF *mordrer*) may be involved. In
fol for *ful* 'full' we may have an instance of *o* instead of *u*, but the ME
spellings are ambiguous because of the common use of *o* for *u* (especially
in the neighbourhood of *n*, *m*, and *u*).

It is not clear whether the spelling *u* for *o* before *ng* is to be explained
as a change of *o* to *u* before a supported nasal or as the result of the
shortening of *ọ̄* (§8). It is attested by rimes such as *among : tung*, and is
Western, but also occurs here and there in the East, as the forms of
Modern Standard English show.

Note 17   Between *w* and *m*, *i* became *u* in *wumman*, *wom(m)an* beside *wimman* (OE *wīfman*) 'woman'. Later, the form with *-i-* became
established as the plural, which had earlier also been *wummen* and
wommen. Similarly, there are some instances of *swumme(n)* for *swimmen*
'to swim'.

Note 18   Finally and before a consonant, *er* became *ar* during the
14th century, first in the North. Spellings of *ar* for *er* appear to an
increasing extent in 15th century MSS, e.g. *starre* for *sterre* 'star', *dark*
for *derk* 'dark', *sarvice*, *marvel*, etc.

Note 19   Spellings of *e* for [ā], *i* or *y* for [ẹ̄], and *ou* for [ọ̄] in 15th
century MSS indicate that the changes of ME [ā] to [ẹ̄], of [ẹ̄] to [ī]
and of [ọ̄] to [ū] have begun. Rimes of ME [ī] with *ui* or *ai* and spelling
of [ī] as *ei* or *ey* show that the diphthongisation of [ī] has begun, and
rimes with words containing the diphthong *ou*, that of [ū].

To what extent ME *ẹ̄* became *ī* early enough to share in the diphthongisation to ModE *ai* is not clear. This development appears in
French loanwords, particularly for Fr. *é* (from Lat. *a* in an open syllable,
§22A), as in ModE *friar*, ME *frere*, and ModE *dice*, ME *de*, pl. *des*; and
for Fr. *ué* (§23.3), in ModE *choir*, ME *cuer*, and in ModE *contrive*, ME
contreue(n); and in one native word, ModE *briar*, ME *brer* (OE *brēr* in
Anglian and Kentish), but cf. Fr. *bruyère*.

Note 20 In Kentish from the 12th century to the 14th, OE *ēa* is spelt *ya*, *yea*, *ye*, and less frequently *e*; and OE *īo* is spelt *ie*, *ye*, and finally *i* or *y*. A diphthongal pronunciation may also have survived longer in Devon, in view of place-names spelt with *ea* or *ya* for OE *ea* and *ēa*.

§12 Lengthening of Short Vowels in Open Syllables

A About the first half of the 13th century—somewhat earlier in the North—the short vowels *a* (including that produced in accordance with §§10 and 11.1), *e* and *o* were lengthened in open syllables, i.e. before single consonants which begin the next syllable, and before consonant groups transferred to the next syllable, such as *st* and a stop followed by a liquid or a nasal.

As a result, *a* became *ā*, *e* became *ę̄*, and *o* became *ǭ*; and these sounds coalesced with other ME long vowels of the same quality, so that *ā* coalesced with OE *ā* kept in the North (§11.4) and French long *ā* (§21); *ę̄* with *ę̄* as in §11.2 and French long *ę̄* (§21); and *ǭ* with Southern *ǭ* from OE *ā* (§11.4) and French long *ǭ* (§21).

We therefore find in ME rimes of N *lathe* (OE *lāþ* 'loathsome') with *bathe* (OE *baþian*); S *more* (OE *māra*) with *bifore* (OE *beforan*); and *bere* (OE *beran* 'to bear') with *ere* (OE *ēare* 'ear').

Note 1 In their later development these sounds differ from close [ẹ̄] and [ọ̄], but not (on the evidence of the modern dialects) from open [ę̄] and [ǭ] of other origins (§11.2 and 4), except in western Yorkshire and southern and central Lancashire, although careful ME poets avoid riming them, except before *r*.

Note 2 The N forms *tak* 'to take', *get* 'to get' (which makes its way into StdE in the 15th century) and *breck* 'to break' either derive their short vowels from OE by-forms with geminates or are forms shortened as in §9.3.

B Lengthening of *i* and *u* to [ẹ̄] and [ọ̄] respectively does not occur until later, and only in some areas, i.e. north of the Humber in the second half of the 13th century and in more southerly districts in the 14th. (In the North final -*e* had meanwhile become silent (§27), so that the conditions for the lengthening existed only before endings made up of *e* plus a consonant, or of suffixes other than -*e*.) Hence: N *sǭnes* pl. 'sons', *sǭmer* 'summer', *ę̄vil*, and *schę̄pes* pl. 'ships', and south of the Humber also *ywrę̄te* 'written' and *lǭve* 'love'. ModE *week*, *wood* and *evil* are due to this lengthening.

Note 3 This lengthening likewise presupposes a more open pronunciation of *i* and *u*, which is indicated by spellings of *e* for *i* even in
closed syllables (see §11, n. 16) and to a lesser extent by spellings of *o*
for *u*, as these also occur otherwise (see §5B).

The lengthening itself is evidenced, apart from infrequent double-
spellings (*ee* and *oo*), particularly in rimes.

North of the Humber the new [ọ] sound shared in the development
to [ü] (§11.6), so that later it is again spelt *u*, or sometimes *ui*.

Note 4 Outside the North, the lengthening is attested in spellings
and rimes in texts from Norfolk and from the South West.

C   Lengthening did not take place: (1) in antepenultimate
syllables—as disyllabic and trisyllabic forms often occurred side
by side in the inflexion of a word, doublets with short and long
root syllables were produced; and sometimes the short vowel,
sometimes the long, was extended to all forms, e.g. *fāper* sg.,
făperes pl.; *hēuen* sg., *hĕuenes* pl.; and *bōdi* sg., *bŏdies* pl.; (2) in
words with reduced sentence stress such as *have* 'to have' and
are 'are'; and (3) as a result of transfer of the short vowel of
monosyllabic inflected forms to disyllabic, as in *stăf* sg., *stăves* pl.,
and *blăk* sg., *blăke* pl. 'black'.

§13 Formation of New Diphthongs in Middle English

A   *Fusion of Vowels with Following Vocalised Palatal ġ*

In OE the vocalisation of *ġ*, which occurred after the front
vowels *æ*, *e* and *i*, had been indicated by occasional spellings
of *i* instead of *g*.

The results of the fusion are as follows:

1. *æġ* became *ai*: OE *dæġ*, ME *dai* 'day'.

2. *eġ* became *ei*, which coalesced with *ai*: OE *weġ*, ME *wei*,
wai 'way'.

3. *ǣġ* became *ei* and then *ai*: OE *cǣġ*, ME *kai* 'key'; WS
grǣġ, ME *grai* 'grey'; and OE *ǣġ*, ME *ei* or *ai* 'egg'.

Note 1 In the second half of the 14th century in parts of the North
(Scotland, Yorkshire), *ai* was monophthongised to *ā*, and from then on
we find rimes of *ā* and *ai* and spellings like *fane* 'glad' (elsewhere in ME
fain, from OE *fæġen*), *fare* 'fair' (elsewhere *fair*, from OE *fæġer*), and
conversely *ai* for *ā*: *maid* 'made'. The same development appears in
Norfolk in the late 15th century.

4. *ēġ* (not only from OE *ē* and *ēo* before *ġ*, but also OE *ē* from
ēa by smoothing) became *ei* and then *ai* at the end of a word or

of a syllable followed by another beginning in a consonant; medially, however, it became *ei* and then *ī* before a syllable which originally began with a vowel, although not everywhere at the same time. Hence ME *grei, grai* from Angl.Kt. *grēġ; hei, hai* 'hay' from OE *hēġ*; pret. *deide, daide* 'died' but inf. *deien, dien* from OE **dēgan; eie, ie* 'eye' from OE *ēaġe, ēġe*; and *leie(n), lie(n)* 'to tell lies' from OE *lēogan*.

Note 2 North of the Humber *ī* from OE *ēġ, ēoġ* is rare; because of the early loss of final -*e*, it could occur only before endings consisting of a vowel plus a consonant; and it was, moreover, removed by levelling.

Note 3 The monophthongisation of *ẹi* to *ī* first took place in the South West at the end of the 12th century in forms derived from OE *ēoġ*; in other parts of England it occurred in the 13th and 14th centuries, and not everywhere at the same time. The diphthong apparently remained longest in Cheshire and Lancashire.

5. *iġ* yielded not a diphthong but *ī*: ME *nīn, nīne* 'nine' from OE *niġon*; ME *stile* from OE *stiġol* 'stile'.

Note 4 North of the Humber *neȝen, neen* ([nīn] in the modern dialects) are also found, because the lengthening of *i* to *ẹ̄* (§12B) preceded the vocalisation of *ġ*. ModE (dialectal) [stīl] for Std [stail] presupposes a similar development.

6. *īġ* yielded *ī*: ME *stien* from OE *stīgan* 'to climb'.

7. *ẏ̄ġ* produced, in accordance with the dialectal development of *ȳ* (§11.5), *ei* later *ai*, or *ẹi* and *ī* in Kent and the South East; *ī* in the North and East; and in the West a sound [üi], spelt *ui*, which was later monophthongised to [ü], spelt *u*. Hence from OE *byġeþ* we have *beieþ*, later *baieþ, bieþ, buieþ, bueþ* 'he buys'; and from OE *drȳġe*, ME *dreie, drie, druie*, and *drue* 'dry'.

B *Fusion of Vowels with* w *or Velar* g [ȝ]

In all of the ME dialects, all vowels fused with a following *w* to form diphthongs in -*u*.

Velar *g* (which appeared after OE *a, o* and *u*) was vocalised, by way of *w*, to *u* and then likewise fused with the preceding vowel to form a diphthong. In the North this vocalisation did not take place until after final -*e* had become silent, and by then velar [ȝ] remained only before endings consisting of *e* plus a consonant (e.g. *el, en*); before silent -*e* it had become final and hence unvoiced to [χ], and so developed as in section C below.

Note 5 Spellings of *w* instead of *ȝ* appear in the South West Midlands about 1200, but not until later in the rest of the country; Kentish
texts keep *ȝ* until 1400. To what extent this reflects the actual pronunciation is doubtful.

The results are as follows:

1. *ag* and *aw* became *au*: OE *strawes* (gen.) became *straues*
generally in ME, whence nom. *straw*; OE *dragan* became ME
drawe(n) 'to draw'; and OE *maga* became ME *mawe* 'maw'.
(The Northern uninflected forms are *dragh* and *magh*.)

2. *āg* and *āw* became *ou* (since *ā* became *ǭ*, §11.4) south of
the Humber, *au* north of it. Hence OE *blāwan* gave ME *blowe*
or *blawe* 'to blow'; OE *cnāwan* gave ME *knowe* or *knawe* 'to
know'; and OE *āgan* gave ME *owe* 'to own' (N uninflected *agh*).

3. *og* became *ou*: ME *bowe* (Northern *bogh*) from OE *boga*
'bow'. (In OE *ow* did not occur.)

4. *ōg* and *ōw* evidently also produced *ou*. But south of the
Humber words with original *ōg* later rime with *ū*, and north of
it the vocalising of [ȝ] did not take place until after the change
of *ǭ* to [ŭ] (§11.6), when there developed a diphthong, spelt *eu*
or *ew*, which probably had the sound [iu], produced by way
of [üu].

Examples with [ou] include ME *blowe(n)*, OE *blōwan* 'to bloom';
ME *glowe(n)*, OE *glōwan* 'to glow'; and those with [ū] include
ME *bowes*, Northern *bewes*, OE *bōgas* pl. 'boughs'; ME *plowes*,
N *plewes*, OE *plōgas* pl. 'ploughs'; and ME *inowe*, N *enewe*, OE
genōge 'enough'.

Note 6 In the last three examples, *ū* for *ōg* may have been transferred from the uninflected forms *bough* (sg.), *plough* (sg.), and *enough*,
whose development follows section C.3 below.

After *w*, the change of *ou* (from *ǭg*) to [ū] is certain in ME *swowenen*,
swoune(n) 'to swoon' from OE **swōgenian*, and ME *wowe(n)* 'to woo'
from OE *wōgian*.

After *f* and [j], *ou* from *ōw* pretty generally changed to *ū*, as in ME
four, *fuwer* 'four' (OE *fēower* with stress-shift) and ME *ȝou*, *ȝu* 'you'
(OE *ēow* with stress-shift).

Note 7 In Kent and parts of the West and North, and perhaps in
the South East too, ME *ou* (except when derived from *ǭg*) became *au*,
as is shown by spellings such as *blawe* 'to blow', *snaw* 'snow' and *fawre*
'four', and rimes like *knawe* 'to know' and *drawe* 'to draw'.

5. *ŭg* yielded *ū*, spelt *ou* or *ow*: ME *foul*, *fowl* 'bird' from
OE *fugol*; ME *bowe(n)* 'to bow' from OE *būgan*.

6. *ǣw* and *ēaw* became *eu*: ME *lewed* 'lay' from OE *lǣwed*; ME *schewe(n)* 'to show' from OE *scēawian*.

Note 8 Beside *schewe(n)*, a frequent form in ME is *schowe(n)*, due to stress-shift in OE.

7. *eow* became *eu*: ME *spewe(n)* 'to spew' from OE *speowian*.

8. *ēow* became *ęu*. This did not coalesce with *eu* from OE *ǣw*, *aw* and *eow*, but evidently became *iu* early in the 14th century, when spellings with *iw* begin to appear, and conversely *iu* from *w* (see 9 below) is spelt *eu* and *ew*. Later there also appear spellings with *uw* and *u*, which are hard to interpret: they indicate either a pronunciation [üu], [ü], or simply coalescence with Fr. [ü] (§23.2b). Hence ME *newe*, *niwe*, and *nuwe* 'new' from OE (Angl.) *nēowe*; ME *trewe*, *triwe* and *truwe* 'true' from OE *rēow*; and ME *knew*, *kniw* and *knuw* 'he knew' from OE *cnēow*.

Note 9 ME *troup* 'truth' beside *trewp* from OE *trēowp* is due to OE stress-shift, and similarly *four* 'four' (OE *fēower*) and *ȝou* 'you' (OE *ēow*).

9. *īw* became *iu*, later also spelt *ew*, *uw*, and *u* (see 8 above): ME *stiward*, *steward* and *stuard* 'steward' (OE *stīȝweard*); ME *iwesday*, *tewesday* and *tuesday* 'Tuesday' (OE *tīwesdæȝ*); and South Western *triwe*, *trewe* and *true* 'true' (WS *trīewe*).

C *Formation of Diphthongs from Glides before* [χ]

The sounds [χ] and [χ'] in OE were, respectively, voiceless velar and palatal spirants, spelt *h*. The development of glides is most evident south of the Humber.

BEFORE VELAR [χ]

1. *a* became *au* by the development of a glide generally in ME, hence *taughte* (OE *tāhte*, with shortening as in §9.1), *slaughter*, N and M *aught* 'eight' (Angl. *æhta* smoothed from *eahta*), N and M *saugh* 'saw' (Angl. *sæh* smoothed from *seah*). In the North there are also forms in which no glide is spelt, e.g. *taght*, *aght*.

Note 10 Beside N and M *aught*, *saugh* the South has *eight*, *seigh*, results of the WS and Kentish smoothing to *ehta* and *seh* (see 6 below).

ā became *ou* south of the Humber (as *ā* became *ǭ*, §11.4); in the North it became *au* or remained without a glide. Hence S *dough*, N *daugh* or *dagh* 'dough' (OE *dāh*).

2. *o* became *ou* by the development of a glide only south of

the Humber and not always there; in the North there is n‹
evidence of diphthongisation. Hence ME *doughter, doghter* (O‖
dohtor); ME *trough, trogh* (OE *troh*); ME *broughte, broghte* (O‖
brōhte, with shortening as in §9.1).

Note 11 Before *ght*, this *ou* changed to *au* sporadically towards th‹
end of the 14th century, as is shown by spellings like *daughter*; thes‹
become more frequent after 1500.

3. *ǭ* became *ou* south of the Humber: *plough* (OE *plōh*), *boug.*
(OE *bōh*), *enough* (OE *genōh*). From the later 14th century thes‹
words rime with *ū*, e.g. with *rough* (OE *rūh*). Whether thi‹
monophthongisation is proper to the forms with [χ], or whethe‹
it involves a transfer of the development in the inflected form‹
(see section B.4 above, and n. 6), cannot be decided. North c‹
the Humber no diphthong developed: hence *bogh, enogh*. Th‹
later Scots forms *eneugh, pleugh* are either spellings of *eu* for [ü̃‹
from *ǭ* (see §§11.6 and 23.2*b*), or have [iu] transferred from th‹
inflected forms (see section B.4 above).

4. *u* seems to have been lengthened; both the ME spelling *o*‹
and the further development suggest this. Examples are M‖
þrough 'through' (OE *þurh*) and *drought*.

5. *ū* remained unchanged, spelt *ou*, as in ME *rough* (OE *rūh*‖

BEFORE PALATAL [χ′]

6. *e* gave *ei*, as in S *eighte* (OE *ehta* from *eahta* with WS an‹
Kentish smoothing, cf. §10, n. 1, para. 4), *seigh* 'saw', *neighebou*‹
(OE *nēahʒebur*, with shortening, §9).

Note 12 On *aught, saugh* (with Anglian smoothing to *æ*), see 1 abov‹
and n. 10.

The *e* produced by smoothing of *eo* before *ht* remained in O‖
only where there was a following back vowel; otherwise it b‹
came *i*. Hence *ei* occurs beside *i* (as in 8 below) in different i‹
flected forms in ME, as in *feight* inf. 'to fight' (OE *feohta*‹
beside *fight* (from the 2nd and 3rd person sg.), which was the‹
generalised.

7. *ę̄* (from OE *ēo* and *ēa* smoothed) south of the Humber gav‹
ęi, which later became *ī*: ME *heigh, high* 'high', OE *hēah*; M‖
þeigh, þigh 'thigh', OE *þēoh*. (The sound *ī*, however, could als‹
come from inflected forms which had voiced [ʒ] instead of fin‹
voiceless [χ′] before an ending beginning with a vowel; see se‹
tion A.4 above.)

North of the Humber *ę̄* remained unaltered, hence *heegh* (beside *heie*, *hie* from the inflected forms). As a result of the early
loss of final *-e* in the North (§27), words which had *ę̄* in OE
before original [ʒ] also remained unaltered, because final [ʒ]
was unvoiced to [χ']; hence *eegh* 'eye' (OE *ēaǵe*). By transfer of
this *ę̄* inflected forms like *een* pl. 'eyes', and in turn uninflected
forms without *gh* like *ee* 'eye', were produced.

Note 13   *ī* for *ei* before [χ'] is, like *ī* for *ęi* from *ēǵ*, first found in the
South West and in forms derived from OE *ēo*; cf. n. 3 above.

8. *i* was probably lengthened; the first indications come not
from ME spelling but from the later development in ModE:
hence *knight* (OE *cniht*), *right* (OE *riht*).

D   *Other Types of Diphthongisation*

1. After *b* and *g* in Kent and other southern districts *ō* (both
ō and *ǭ*) sometimes became *uo* as in *guod* 'good', *guos* 'goose' [ǭ]
and *guo* 'to go', *buon* 'bone' [ǭ].

2. In the South West in the 14th century, initial *ō* sometimes
became *wó*, spelt *wo*, as in *wold* 'old', *wotes* 'oats', *won* 'one', and
initial *ē* became *ié*, spelt *ye*, as in *yerthe* 'earth', *yer* 'ear'.

3. In some areas *a* before [š] or [dž] became *ai*, and *e* before
[š] became *ei*: hence *waischen* 'to wash', *chainge* 'to change', and
fleisch 'flesh'. A similar explanation is probable for sporadic *ei*
from *e* before the palatal groups *nct*, *ngd*, and *ngþ*, as in eME
dreint 'drowned' and *streinðe* 'strength' and later ME *seind*
'singed' (p.p. of *singen*, *sengen*).

NORSE ELEMENT

§14   The settlement — which lasted several centuries — of
Norsemen (Danes, Norwegians, and probably Swedes) also in
Eastern, Northern and North Western England led to not only
the adoption of numerous loanwords but also a partial assimilation of English words to Norse phonology. The two languages
were still so much alike that the two races could understand
each other at need, although the sounds of individual words
were often different.

§15   The adoption of Norse loanwords took place in OE, but
the number of them in the extant lOE documents is very limited,
because most of these texts are in West Saxon, and the South
West was the part of England least exposed to Norse influence.
The range of the borrowings therefore only becomes clear in

ME, when numerous texts from Eastern and Northern England
are also preserved.

§16 To what extent Norse loanwords exhibit East Norse
(Danish and Swedish) or West Norse (Norwegian) forms is not
easy to decide, and often quite impossible. At the time of the
occupation of England the dialects of North Germanic did not
differ markedly, and substantial texts in these languages are
extant only from a much later period, so that it is not possible
to make comparisons.

As compared with OE, however, the Norse tongues exhibit
common characteristics, due to their different linguistic develop
ment. These are significant, in individual instances, for estab
lishing whether a Norse borrowing is involved. For the stressed
vowels the following, among others, are noteworthy:

Gmc *ai* becomes *ā* in OE (*ǣ* with *i*-mutation), but in NGmc it wa
probably still *ai* in the Viking period; later it gives ON *ei*, and in Danish
from c.1050, *ē*. Hence OE *hāl*, ME *hāl* or *hǭl* (§11.4), compared with
ME *hail* from ON *heil* 'hale'; ME *haipen* 'heathen' from Norse, compared
with *hēpen* (with *i*-mutation); ME *leip* from Norse beside *lāp*, *lǭp* 'loath
some'.

Gmc *ę̄* is WGmc *ā*, which becomes WS and East Angl. *ǣ*, otherwise
in OE; in NGmc *ā*, which remains. Hence ME *ę̄r*, *ę̄r* 'ere' beside *ār*, *ǭ*
(§11.4) from Norse.

Gmc *au* becomes *ēa* in OE but remains in ON, and later becomes *ou*
or (before [χ]) *ō*. Hence ME *pogh*, *pough* (from ON *poh* with shortening
and in accord with §13C.2), beside *pagh*, *paugh*, *peigh* 'though' (from OE
pēah with shortening, and in accord with §13C.1 and 6).

§17 Stressed Norse vowels which had OE equivalents wer
replaced by them, and had the same phonological development
(§§8-13) from the time of borrowing. These are:

Short Vowels

a as in *flat* 'flat', *hap* 'chance'; with lengthening (§8): *wrāng*, *wrǫn*
'wrong', *wānd*, *wǫnd* 'wand', *bānd*, *bǫnd* 'bond'; and with lengthenin
(§12): *tāke(n)* 'to take', *kāste(n)* 'to throw'.

e as in *brenne(n)* 'to burn' (in place of OE *biernan*, *beornan*); with
lengthening (§12): *gēte(n)* 'to get' (in place of OE *ġietan*, *ġetan*); with
from *i*-mutation in ON: *egg* 'egg', *gest* 'guest' (in place of OE *ġiest*, *ġest*
leg 'leg'.

i as in *skin* 'skin', *skill* 'skill'.

o as in *scot* 'tribute'; with lengthening (§12): *scōre* 'score'.

u as in *sculle* 'skull', *scrubbe(n)* 'scrub'.

y as in *brunie* [ü], *brinie* 'byrnie'; *stunten* [ü], *stenten*, *stinten* 'to stop

Long Vowels

$\bar{a}$ (with further development according to §11.4) as in $w\check{a}n$, $w\varrho n$ 'hope'; $\bar{a}$, $fr\bar{\varrho}$ 'fro' (in place of OE $fram$, $from$); and also for later ON ϱ developed y u-mutation: $ware(n)$, $wore(n)$ 'they were'.

$\bar{e}$ as in $seer$ 'different'.

$\bar{\imath}$ as in $pr\bar{\imath}ve(n)$ 'prosper', $t\bar{\imath}pende$ 'news'.

$\bar{o}$ as in $root$ 'root', $bloome$ 'bloom', $boon$ 'boon'.

$\bar{u}$ as in $droupe(n)$ 'droop'.

$\bar{y}$ as in $pruste(n)$, $priste(n)$ 'to thrust', ski 'sky'.

§18   Of the vowels surviving in ON but not in OE, ai (later ei oalesced with ME ai from §13A.1-3: thus $hail$ 'hale', $greipe(n)$ to prepare'; but ei was monophthongised to [ẹ̄] about 1400 in he group eik, which existed only in Norse words, hence ME eik, later $week$ 'weak', $steik$, later $steek$ 'steak'; ON ey (Gmc au ith i-mutation) similarly coalesced with ai, ei as in $traisten$ to trust'; and ON au was adopted as $\bar{o}$, au and ou: ME $windoʒe$ window' (ON $vindauga$), ME los, $laus$, $lous$ 'loose' (ON $lauss$); IE $gook$, $gauk$, $gouk$ 'cuckoo' (ON $gaukr$).

FRENCH (AND LATIN) ELEMENT

§19   French loanwords adopted in English after the Norman Conquest usually have the forms of Northern French (Norman-Picard), specifically those of its insular (Anglo-Norman) variant, nd not until after 1300 are some Central French forms borrowed. In addition, there is a group of loanwords borrowed directly from Latin or in forms only slightly assimilated to those f French.

§20   Stress

The borrowings are made to conform to the stress-system of he native element of the language. The strongest and most mphatic stress falls on the first syllable, unless this is a weak prefix. Occasionally, then, French pretonic syllables become onic and tonic syllables become post-tonic, although to what xtent the latter have already been reduced in ME can only arely be determined from the written forms (see §31B). ME poets use French tonic syllables, which are unstressed in later English, to carry the rime, as in $pité$, $honóur$, $batáile$; this suggests that a perceptible secondary-stress was still given to these yllables at least on occasion.

c

§21 Vowel Quantity

The length of French vowels stressed in accordance with th
English system usually conforms to the normal types of syllable
length in native words, although there are occasional variation:

1. Final vowels are long.

2. In disyllables, and in words having the stress on the pen
ultimate syllable (and an unstressed prefix), long vowels appea
before single consonants, before a stop or spirant followed b
a liquid, and before *st* (i.e. in open syllables, cf. §12): hence M
māle, blāme, escāpen, douten, cāge, āche, poudre, tāble, hāst
cōaste etc.; likewise in French pretonic syllables which ai
stressed in English, as in *bāsin, bācoun*; and in Latin word
irrespective of the Latin quantity, e.g. *tīgre, mētre, sācren* 't
hallow', etc.

Sometimes, however, the consonant is doubled and the vow
of the stressed syllable is then short, as in *robben, cacchen, pledg*
lettre, suffre(n), and there are also alternative forms, such a
presse and *prēce, dette* and *dēte* 'debt', *rocche* and *rōche* 'rock
dobble and *double, trobble* and *trouble*. Short vowels occur, more
over, in words which probably kept the stress longer on the fina
syllable, such as *cĭté* or *cĭty, prĭson, băron* or *băroun, pĭté* or *pĭt*
mŭton, plěsaunt, hěron, and in Latin words, such as *frĭgid, lĭqui*
etc.

3. Before groups of consonants except *st* and those consistin
of a stop or spirant followed by a liquid—i.e. in syllables whic
are closed in English (§12)—short vowels are normal, as in *ten*
'time', *defenden, membre, simple, test, part, arme* 'weapon', an
in Latin words such as *apt, adde(n), desk, correct, prince, conflic*
etc., but long vowels also occur before some consonant group
as in *pę̄rle* 'pearl', *tę̄rme*, in the North in *pārt* (Scots *pairt, c*
§5, n. 5), *ārt*, and in many districts in *scārce*.

4. Before single final consonants in monosyllables, long vowe
are usual, as in *pās* 'step', *clę̄r* 'clear', *strīf* 'strife' and *prīs* 'price
but short vowels appear when the final consonant is doubled
as in *track* and in *butt* 'target', and there are alternative form
such as *bę̄k* and *beck* 'beak'.

5. Initial syllables of trisyllables, stressed in English, ai
short, hence *lăvendre, vĭnegar, pŭnishe(n), mătere, mĕmory, mĭ*
ery, lĕgible, nătural, crĭminal, ămorous, rĕgular, vĭsage, etc., b

ong vowels appear when the second syllable consists of a vowel
ollowed by another, as in *pātient, nātioun, rēgioun, cūrious*, or
n *glōrie, stōrie* (cf. §23, n. 4); in syllables followed by another
beginning with a vowel, as in *pōete, dīete* and *dīamaund*; and
often in syllables before the suffix *-able*, as in *vōcable* and *cāpable*
but not in *prŏbable*).

Note In 14th and 15th century texts sporadic *ę̄* for *i* (lengthened in
open syllables, §12B) appears, as in *pete, presoun*, and *vesage*, in the short
yllables referred to in 2 and 5 above, after the loss of final *-e*.

§22 Stressed ME Equivalents of French and Latin Vowels

French vowels which have English equivalents coalesce with
hem. These are:

A Common OF Vowels

The short vowels *a, e, i, o, u*; the long vowels *ā, ū* (spelt *ou*);
nd the diphthongs *ai, au*, and *ou*. OF long *ē* coalesced with
ME *ę̄*, as in *beste* 'beast' (VL *besta*; CL *bestia*) and *feste* (Lat.
festa), except that OF *é* derived from Lat. *a* in an open syllable
coalesced with ME *ę̄*, as in *gre* 'pleasure' (Lat. *gratum*) and *de*
(Lat. *datum*). OF long *ō* coalesced with ME *ǭ*, as in *hǭst* 'host',
ǭste 'side', *rǫche* 'rock', *rǫbe*, and *clǫse(n)*; but in the neighbour-
ood of labials ME *ǭ* also is found, as in *fool, boote, poovre* 'poor'
but *pǭste, suppǭsen*). (AN had no close *o*; this sound has become
ι, see section B below.)

Note 1 On lME *ī* for *ę̄* from Lat. *a*, cf. §11, n. 19.
Note 2 Diphthongs ending in *-u* were monophthongised after the
nd of the 13th century, except in the North West and North, before
abials, [tš], [dž], [š] and [ž], with loss of the *u* and lengthening of the
irst element. Hence *safe* for *saufe* 'safe', *chafen* 'to warm oneself' (OF
chauffer), *bame* 'balm', *pame* 'palm', *cope(n)* from *coupe(n)* 'to hit', *rēme*
realm' from *reume* (OF *reaume*, cf. §23.8), *limenour* 'illuminator' (from
illumenour; with *i* from *iu* for [ü], as in §23.2*b*, unless *ü* was replaced
y *i*, as in §23, n. 2), *sage* 'sage (the plant)', **Becham* for *Beauchamp*,
odier for *soudier* 'soldier', and *solysion* for *solucion* 'solution'.

B Anglo-Norman By-forms

1. *a* before a nasal (*n, m*) in the same syllable is spelt *au*,
from the 13th century, in both AN and contemporary English
exts, and this *au* coalesces with *au* of other origins; hence
aunde 'meadow', *demaunde(n), graunte(n), daunse(n)* 'to dance',

chaunce, aungel 'angel', *chaumbre, laumpe*. But before *ng, n*
spellings with *au* are uncommon, and the usual forms are e.g
jangle(n) 'to jest', *flank*. Before *mb* and [ndž], spelt *nge, au*
spellings become less frequent during the 14th century, and ii
these positions the later development—except in some Northern
and North Western dialects—is a continuation of ME *ā*, as ii
chamber, angel, change. This is not so with *braunch* 'branch'
which has [ntš].

Note 3 The monophthongisation of *au* to *ā* before *mb* and [ndž]
corresponds to that affecting diphthongs ending in *-u* before labials
[tš], [dž], [š] and [ž]; see n. 2 above.

2. *en* did not become *an* in AN as in CF, but remained dis
tinct, hence *entente* 'intention', *emperour*, and *defendre*.

3. *o* (from both VL *ǫ* and *ọ*) before a supported nasal is *u* ii
AN (spelt *o* or *u*, and also *ou* when long), *o* in CF; hence MI
numbre, nombre, noumbre 'number', *frunt* or *front* 'forehead'
mount, count, profound, and the prefix *cun-, con-*.

4. *ǫ, u*, later spelt *ou* (VL *ǫ* in French stressed open and clos
syllables before oral consonants, and in French pretonic syl
lables) is always *u* (spelt *o* or *u*, and *ou* when long) in AN, henc
cup, disturben, duble or *double, tour* 'tower', *doute(n)* 'to doubt'
flour 'flower' and *culour* or *colour*.

Note 4 It is not easy to explain ME *ō* instead of the expected *ū* ii
prove(n) and *move(n)*, which derive from OF forms *prouver, prouvons*
mouvoir, mouvons, stressed on the ending, alongside ME *preue(n), meve(n)*
derived from forms stressed on the root-syllable, cf. § 23.3.

5. *ai* and *ei* coalesced in AN. In borrowings into English
doubtless under the influence of contemporary AN phonology
the diphthong (ME *ai*) remains finally, before a nasal, and be
fore *r*, but has usually been monophthongised to ME [ę̄
before dentals. Hence : *rai* 'ray', *assai* 'test', *paie(n)* 'to pay', *air*
paire, affaire (beside *affere*), *vain, remaine(n), plainte, preie(n)*
praie(n) 'to pray', *faire, eir, air* 'heir', *veile*; but *pes* 'peace', *es*
'ease', *sesen* 'to seize', *fet* 'deed', *resoun, plesaunt, plesir* 'pleasure'
egle 'eagle', and *pese* 'pea'.

Note 5 CF *oi* from older *ei* (kept in AN), derived from VL *ę* ii
stressed open syllables, is infrequent in borrowings into English, bu
appears in *avoir* 'property', *coy, royal, voyage* and a few other words.

Note 6 On the Northern monophthongisation of *ai*, cf. § 13, n. 1.

6. *ie* (VL *ę* in stressed open syllables) became *e* in AN from about the 12th century and coalesced with ME [ē], hence ME *ref*, *greef* 'grief', *breef* 'brief', *fevre* 'fever', *fer*, *fers* 'fierce', *peece* 'piece' and *neece* 'niece'. The spelling *ie*, from CF, does not appear in MSS until the 15th century.

7. In AN, vowels before palatalised [l'] and [n'] became diphthongs ending in *i* as a result of the loss of the palatalisation; these diphthongs coalesced with others in -*i* of different origin. Hence ME *faile(n)*, *assaile(n)*, *bataile*, *gaine(n)*, *reine(n)* 'to reign', *feine(n)* 'to feign', *pleine(n)* or *plaine(n)* 'to complain', *soil* (OF *ouillir*).

Note 7 In Scots we find—probably in imitation of CF pronunciation—a simple vowel before [lj], spelt *lȝ*, and [nj], spelt *nȝ*, as in *batalȝe*, *assalȝe*, *falȝe*, *fenȝe*, *ganȝe*. In the 15th century these forms also appear in the South, as in *talie* beside *taile* 'tally', *rally* beside *rail* 'to tease', *ully* beside *soil*, *onion* beside *oinon*, and *spaniel* beside *spainel*.

§23 French vowels which did not occur in English, or only in some dialects, were treated as follows:

1. French nasalised vowels were replaced by the corresponding oral vowels.

2. [ü], spelt *u*:

(*a*) The sound [ü], shortened as described in §21, was replaced by [u]—although spellings with *o*, otherwise common for [u], are rare—and so did not coalesce with [ü] from OE *y* (later replaced by *i*) preserved in the West and South West. Hence ME *judgen*, also *jodge* 'to judge', *just*, *humble*, and *studie(n)*, *study*, *stody* 'to study'.

Note 1 Apparently because it was borrowed earlier, OF *hurter* 'to hurt' exhibits the dialectal development of OE *y* seen in §11.5, hence ME *hurte(n)*, *hirte(n)*, *herte(n)*.

(*b*) The sound [ǖ], long in terms of §21, coalesced in the West and South West with native [ǖ] from OE *ȳ* (§11.5) and in the North with [ǖ] from OE *ō̜* (§11.6); both French [ǖ] rimes with these sounds. Later, however, whereas in the North Fr. [ǖ] and [ǖ] from OE *ō̜* have the same development, in the West and South West native [ǖ] is replaced by *i* (§11.5) but [ǖ] in French words is not. In the rest of England an attempt seems to have been made to retain the distinctive pronunciation of French [ǖ], but in the 14th century it frequently coalesced with ME *iu* (from OE *ēow* and *īw*, §13B.8, 9), as can be seen from spellings of *ew*

for OF [ǖ] and *u* or *uw* for ME *iu*. Whether the result of the
coalescence was [iu], [üu] or [ü] cannot be determined. Hence
ME *glu*, later also *glew* 'glue', *duke* or *deuke*, *use*(*n*), *refuse*(*n*)
rude and in the North also *roide* (with *oi* for *ō*, §5, n. 5).

Note 2   Here and there Fr. [ǖ] was replaced by ME [ū], as can be
inferred from spellings like *douk*, *joupe* 'skirt' (OF *jupe*) and rimes like
nature : *emperour*; this seems to have been not a regional but a lower
class rendering of the French sound. Spellings of *ou* for [ü] occur in
some AN MSS as well. There are also, apparently, some spellings of [ü]
especially when unstressed, as *i*.

3. *ué* (VL stressed *ǫ* in open syllables), which became first
[uö] and then [ö] in French from the 13th century, appears to
have become mostly [ö] in AN already in the 12th. In English
it is unrounded to [e] or [ē], like native [ö] from OE *eo* (§10);
this unrounding occurs later in the West Midlands and the South
than elsewhere. Spellings with *ue* are rare, and (as in AN MSS
eo is usual, beside *o* and *u*, and later *e* or *ee*: thus we have *prueven*
pruven, *preve*(*n*) 'to prove' (alongside *proven*, §22, n. 4), *beef*
peple or *people*.

Note 3   After *k* the *u* remains, hence ME *queor*, *quer* 'choir' (OF *cue*
from Lat. *chorus*).

4. *oi* (Lat. or Gmc *au* plus epenthetic *i*) is adopted in English
as *oi*, as in *joie* 'joy', *noise*, *cloistre*, and *chois*. CF *oi* (instead of
AN *ei*) in later borrowings coalesces with this sound; see §22, n. 5

Note 4   Instead of CF *gloire*, *memoire*, *estoire*, the prevalent English
forms are *glorie*, *memorie*, *storie* (from AN), which are closer to the
original Latin forms of these words.

5. *ui* (VL *ǫ* plus epenthetic *i*) in AN does not coalesce with *o*
from the 13th century as in CF, but remains distinct. In English
borrowings the spelling *oi* occurs beside *ui*, but the two sounds
did not coalesce in ME because of their long-standing separate
development. Hence we have ME *puint* or *point* 'point', *poison*
but (with CF *oi*) *voice* and *toile*(*n*).

Note 5   Before [š] and [ž] a later monophthongisation occurs, as in
bushel and *crushe*(*n*).
   Cross, beside Fr. *croiss*, is a Norse or Irish borrowing.
   In the North, as in *ai* to *ā* (§13, n. 1), *oi* is monophthongised to *ǭ* and
ui to *ū*, in the second half of the 14th century; hence, particularly in
Scots, *chos* 'choice', *nose* 'noise', *jo* 'joy', *vos* 'voice' and *punt* 'point'
This is the explanation also of the spellings *oi* for *ō* and *ui* for *ū* (§5, n. 5

6. [üi] (VL *u* plus epenthetic *i*) was often monophthongised to *ü* in AN, so that beside *ui* one finds spellings with *u* and also *u* (§23.2*b*), as in *fruit, frut, freut* 'fruit'; [üi] also rimes with [ü]. Before [š] there is shortening, and [ü] becomes [u] (§22.2*a*), as in *cusshen* 'cushion' and *ussher* 'usher'.

7. *ieu* became AN *iu*, as in *riule* 'rule', *jiw* 'Jew', later spelt *u* as well (cf. §13B.9), as in *reule*, *jew*.

8. *eau* became *eu*, and before a labial (cf. §22, n. 2) *ę̨*, hence *reume*, later *reme* 'realm', and the personal names **Becham* for *Beauchamp*, *Bemont* for *Beaumont*.

Vowels of Unstressed Syllables

§24 OE Short Vowels in Post-tonic Syllables

OE *a*, *o* and *u* finally and in inflexions became, in the 10th and 11th centuries, a sound spelt at first variously and then *e*. OE *æ* and *i* in these positions had already become *e* early in OE.

Accordingly, one still finds in ME in final syllables, apart from *e*, only the following:

i in the post-tonic syllables -*isch* (e.g. *englisch*), -*ing* (e.g. *schilling* and in verbal nouns in -*ing*), -*inde* (Southern ending of the pres.ptc., §68), -*liche* (-*ly*), and -*y* (OE -*iġ*).

Note 1   Early in ME the ending -*ung* in verbal nouns was replaced by -*ing*, and appears only in some early South Western texts.

o in the suffix -*ok* (from OE -*uc*), e.g. *bullok* 'bullock', and in loanwords such as *abbot* and *bishop*.

u before *m*, as in *bosum* 'bosom', and in the derivative suffix -*sum*, as in *longsum* 'slow', *buhsum* or *buxum* 'obedient'.

Note 2   On the Northern pres.ptc. ending -*and*, cf. §68.
Note 3   In place of *e*, *i* (*y*) is written in the endings -*es*, -*eth*, -*en*, -*er*, -*el*, and -*ed* from the 13th century at first in Northern and later in Southern texts as well, as in *wallis* 'walls', *bindith* 'he binds', *kitchin* 'kitchen', *fadir* 'father', *mekil* 'large' and *askid* 'asked'.
Towards the end of the 14th century and in the 15th, first of all in West Midland MSS and in the later 15th century also in MSS from other parts of the Midlands except the East, the spelling in the above endings is *u* instead of *e*, e.g. *werkus*, *fadur*, *modur*, and *askud*.

§25 Long Vowels in Post-tonic Syllables

Long vowels in post-tonic syllables had already been short
ened to some extent in OE; where they remained, shortening
took place in ME, as in compounds with -*dōm* (*wisdom, kingdom*)
-*wīs* (*rightwis*), -*rēde* and -*līche*; in the suffix -*ī* from OE -*iġ* (*hali*
holi 'holy'); and in words with weak sentence stress (*þu* from
þou, etc.).

§26 Development of New Unstressed Vowels

In ME parasitic vowels develop from syllabic OE *l*, *n* and *r*
and also between *r* or *l* and [ʒ], [χ] and *w*, although not uni
versally before [χ] and *w*. Hence ME *setel* 'seat' (OE *setl*), *house*
'the Eucharist' (OE *hūsl*), *taken* or *token* 'token' (OE *tācn*), *ake*
or *akir* 'acre' (OE *æcr*); *borewe* or *borowe* 'to borrow' (OE *borgian*)
burewe, *burowe* or *borough* (OE *burh*, *burg-*), *swalewe* or *swalow*
'swallow' (OE *swalwe*, *swealwe*), and *þorough*, *þoru* 'through' (OE
þurh), but also *galwe*, *burgh*, and *þurgh*.

§27 Loss of Final -*e*

Final -*e* gradually disappeared, from the 12th century, first
in words with weak sentence stress such as *þan* 'then' (for *þane*)
whan or *when*, and *but* or *bot*; later, but still in the 12th century
in trisyllables with a long first syllable (Orrm already has *laffdi*
for OE *hlǣfdiġe* 'lady'); and the remaining instances (in tri
syllables with a short first syllable, and in disyllables) disappeared
in the North in the 13th century and in the South gradually
during the 14th.

Note   Apart from spellings, the evidence for the loss of final -*e* come
from rimes of words which etymologically had final -*e* with words which
did not. The loss is less evident in metre, because only exact poets avoi
using disyllabic theses. Chaucer, writing in London in the second hal
of the 14th century, uses or omits final -*e* according to the demands o
metre; Midland poets omit it already in the first half of the century
Northern poets even earlier, about 1300.
    After the loss of final -*e* the length of a vowel before a single consonan
is often indicated by a suffixed, unetymological -*e*, but in the 15th cen
tury -*e* is written even after double consonants, quite meaninglessly.

§28   Muting of Vowels in Inflexions

About the same time as the loss of final -*e*, although probably
a little later, the vowels in the inflexions -*es*, -*eth* and -*ed* were
lost, first in trisyllables after continuants (e.g. the plurals *fishers*,
beggers, *lovers*) and not until the 15th century in disyllables as
well (e.g. the plurals *clerks* and *bers*; and *takþ* 'he takes'). But
this syncope is only rarely reflected in the written forms.

§29   Syncope in Medial Syllables and Weakly Stressed
Words

A   The loss of unstressed vowels when words are combined
continues OE practice, as in OE *nam* 'I am not' for *ne am*; *nis*
'it is not' for *ne is*; *næs* 'it was not' for *ne wæs*; and *nylle* 'I will
not' for *ne wille*. In ME the final -*e* of the definite article may
be dropped before a noun which begins with a vowel, as in
theffect and *themperour*, and likewise the -*o* of the prep. *to* before
an infinitive, as in *tamende* for *to amende*. But again the loss is
not always expressed in writing.

B   Medially, unstressed vowels are dropped:

1. After vowels, or diphthongs newly developed in ME (§13),
as in ME *fain* (OE *fægen*), *maister* 'master' (OE *mægester*), *four*
(OE *féower*), *saul(e)* or *soul(e)* 'soul' (OE *sāwol*), *youth* (OE *geogoþ*),
and in inflexions like the plurals *dais* beside *dayes*, *wais* beside
wayes.

2. Between consonants, medial syllables after a long first syllable had already been syncopated in OE (as in the pret. *cēpte*
of *cēpan* 'to keep'), and also, although not universally, before *l*
and *r* (as in the plurals *yfle* 'evils' and, in Northumbrian, *reglas*
'rules'); in ME syncope is common in compounds like *Sunday*
(from *sunnenday*), *kindom* 'kingship' (OE *cynedom*), and *neigh-*
bour (from *nehhebur*; OE *nēahgebur*); after a nasal, *l* or *r*, as in
munkes, pl. of *munuk* 'monk' (and consequently also sg. *munk*),
forlorne from *forlorene* 'forlorn', *iborne* from *geborene* 'born'; and,
with a stop inserted between *m* and *r*, in ME *slumbren* 'to slum-
ber' (OE *slumerian*).

Note   When unusual consonant combinations result, syncope does
not occur, and an -*n*- is inserted into the medial syllable on the analogy
of other formations, e.g. *nightingale* from OE *nihtegale*.

§30 OE Pretonic Syllables

In ME in pretonic syllables:

OE *e* became *i* in the OE prefixes *be-* or *bi-* and *ge-*, ME *bi-*
and *i-*, e.g. ME *bifore* (OE *beforan*), *iwis* (OE *ǧewis*);

OE *o* in the prefixes *on-*, *ond-* and *of-* became *a* in ME with
loss of the consonants, hence ME *aboute*, *again*, *amonge*, *anoon*
'immediately' (OE *on ān*) and *adrad* 'afraid' (from OE *ofdrǣdan*);

OE *y* in the prefix *ymbe-* is *u* in ME, hence *umbiloke* 'to look
around', *umbilappe* or *umlappe* 'to embrace'. The Kentish and
Western form is *emb-*, *embe-* (likewise lWS).

§31 Unstressed Vowels in French Words

We deal here with vowels which became unstressed in English, as well as originally unstressed vowels.

A Unstressed post-tonic *-e* was treated as in English words
(§27).

B Vowels which were stressed in French but post-tonic in
English kept their original quantity and quality while at least
a secondary stress remained. Only in MSS of the later 14th and
15th centuries do we find spellings which indicate reduction,
and these attest shortening of long vowels, as in *honur* for *honour*,
and *muttun* or *mutton* for *mutoun*; the change of [ü] to *i* or *e*, as
in *auntir* or *aunter* for *aventure* 'adventure'; that of *i* to *e*, as in
gentel for *gentil*, and *marter* for *martir* 'martyr'; that of *ai* to *i*
or *e*, as in *grammer* for *grammaire* 'grammar', *counsel* for *counceil*
'council', *palis* for *palais* 'palace', and *curtes* for *curteis* 'courtly';
that of [üi] to *i*, as in *condit* for *conduit* 'conduct'; and, in the
later 15th century, that of *é* to *i*, as in *city* for *citee*.

Note 1 Apart from *e*, *ee* (as in *journee*, *countree*), French *ée* from
Lat. *-ata* appears in ME as *eie*, *aie*, *ey* and *ay* in *journeie*, *journey* 'journey'
and *countreie*, *countray* 'country'.

C Syncope in medial syllables occurred as in English words
(§29), but was often prevented by analogy with related words,
hence *citizen* because of *cite*, *city*, and *prisoner* because of *prisoun*.

D Unstressed pretonic vowels were possible in French loanwords, because of the heavy stress on the first syllable, only
in weak prefixes (§20). In an earlier stratum of loanwords
these were definitely not adopted thus for *e* before *s* plus a
consonant, ME has *s-*, as in *stat* for OF *estat* 'state', *stomak*

'stomach', *strif* 'strife', *sprit* 'spirit' (*spirit* is a learned borrowing from Lat. *spiritus*), *spous* 'spouse' and *scrivain* 'scribe'; for *a-*, ME has *mende(n)* for OF *amender* 'to amend'; and for *de-*, ME has *fende* for OF *defendre* 'to defend'.

It was not until a later stratum of loanwords that these unstressed prefixes were adopted, or restored on the model of French or Latin, as in ME *espie* beside *spie* 'to spy', *escape(n)* beside *scape(n)*, *defende* beside *fende*, *entent* 'intention', *consenten*, *releef* 'relief', *errect*, *eternal*, *proceede*, etc.

Note 2 Pretonic vowels before other vowels had already been lost in AN, hence AN and ME *sure*, OF *seure* 'sure'; AN and ME *age*, OF *eage* 'age' (Lat. *secūrum*, *aetātem*).

PART 2   CONSONANTS

§32   Semivowels

1. OE *w* initially is retained: *water*, *wey* 'way', *wonder*, *wlatsum* 'horrible', *wlite* 'countenance', *wrath*, *wroth*, and *wrake* 'vengeance'.

Medially, it remains after consonants (*dwell*, *twelf*), but is lost when followed by *u* (*suster* 'sister' from OE *sweoster*, *swuster*; *such* and *soch* 'such', cf. §11.5) and later also by *ǭ* (*soote* for *swoote* 'sweet', §47); after vowels it was vocalised and fused with the preceding vowel into diphthongs in *-u* (§13B).

Finally, *w* had been vocalised to *u* already in OE, which fused with preceding vowels to form diphthongs in *-u* (§13B).

Note 1 In Northern English (including Scots) and apparently in parts of the East (Norfolk and its environs) *w* seems to have become a bilabial spirant, spelt *v*, as in *vis* 'wise', *vater* 'water' and *dvell* 'to dwell', unless these are simply conventional spellings. Conversely, *w* appears for *v*, as in *lewis* 'he lives', *gewis* 'he gives', *wenim* 'venom', and *wengeaunce*.

French *w* in Gmc loanwords was adopted as *w*, as in Northern French, hence *war*, *wardrobe*, *waste(n)*, *wicket*; but *gide* 'guide', *gile* 'guile' and *gise* 'guise' also occur (the spelling *gu*, as in *guide*, being found first in MSS from the close of the 15th century).

From the 13th century, the usual spelling of OE *cw* is *qu*, as in *quakien* or *quake(n)*, *quelle* 'to kill', and *queen*. French *qu* continued to denote [kw], as in *quantitee*, *conquere(n)* and *questioun*, except before *o* or *u*, hence *coy* 'quiet' (Lat. *quietus*) and *likour* 'liquor'.

Until the beginning of the 13th century, the usual spelling of
OE *hw* was *hw*; later it was *wh* in the South, *qu*, *qw* in the North,
North Midlands and Norfolk, and also *quh* and *qwh* in Scotland;
hence S *what*, N *qwat*, *quhat* etc. 'what'.

Note 2   In Southern and Midland MSS *w* is found for *wh* in words
with weak sentence stress, as in *wat* for *what*, *wile* for *while*.   In alliter-
ative verse from southern districts *wh* and *w* do sometimes alliterate, in
that from northern areas *hw* and *cw* or *qu* alliterate, as in *quartir* 'quarter'
and *whete* 'wheat'.

2. Gmc [j] remains, spelt *ʒ* or *y*: *ʒer*, *yeer* 'year', *ʒoke*, *yoke*
'yoke', *ʒong*, *ʒung* 'young'.

§33   Liquids

l is generally retained, but drops before [tš] in *ech* 'each',
suche, *soche* 'such', *hwuch*, *which* 'which'.

r remains; before *s*, however, occasional assimilation to *ss*
occurs, as in *hoss* for *hors* 'horse'.

Note   Metathesis of *r* is more frequent in ME than OE, partly as a
result of the spread of instances which in OE were confined to certain
areas; hence *þruh* and *through* beside *þurh* and *thorough*, *brid* beside *bird*,
gers beside *gras* and *gres* 'grass', *fresh* beside *fersh*, *therd* beside *thridde*
'third'; and, probably owing to Norse influence, *renne(n)* for OE *iernan*,
yrnan 'to run', *brenne(n)* for OE *beornan* 'to burn', and *bresten* for OE
berstan 'to burst'.

§34   Nasals

m remains in ME.

n remains except when final in weakly stressed words like the
prepositions *in* and *on*, and in the indefinite article *an* and *on*
followed by a word beginning with a consonant.

On final *-n* in inflexions see chapter III below.

Note 1   Before *g* and *k* there was probably a guttural nasal instead
of *n*; the usual spelling is *n*, and only very rarely do scribes seek to
indicate the guttural pronunciation by writing *ng*, as in *dringke* 'to drink'.

Note 2   On the replacement of palatalised Fr. [l'] and [n'], cf. §22B.7
and n. 7.

§35   Labial and Dental Stops

p, *t*, *b*, and *d* generally remain unchanged in ME.

There is widespread unvoicing of final *d* in the ending (-*ed*, -*d*)
of the weak pret.ptc.   Unvoicing also occurs in the West Mid-

lands at the end of a stressed syllable after *n*, *r* or *l*, as in *wint* for *wind* 'wind', *lont* for *lond* 'land', and *bert* for *berd* 'beard'. Unvoicing was perhaps earlier, though, and more widespread than spelling indicates. Corresponding forms with *p* for *b* are uncommon.

Between a nasal and *l* or *r* a stop is occasionally inserted as a bridge, as in *spindle*, *thimbel* beside *thimel* 'thimble', and *empti*.

§36   Labial and Dental Spirants

Initially, voiceless spirants were voiced in the South but retained in the Midlands and North. This is reflected in spelling only for *f* (and *s*, cf. §37) and not for [š] and *þ*, as distinctive letters for the corresponding voiced sounds were lacking. Hence S or SW *veder*, *vader* 'father', *vive* 'five', *vox* 'fox', and *vlesch* 'flesh'. The only other instances of initial *v* are in French words, such as *vain* and *veil*.

Note 1   Spellings of *v* for initial OE *f* are maintained most regularly in Kentish documents. In the South Western texts of the 'Katherine-Group' (from the first half of the 13th century) *v* is found after vowels and voiced consonants, *f* after voiceless consonants. Isolated instances of *v* still occur in otherwise Standard texts of the 15th century, but in general they become less frequent from the 14th century, by assimilation to the Northern forms. As French loanwords do not share in the voicing, it must belong to the OE period, but it could not be expressed in spelling then for lack of a distinctive letter to indicate the voiced spirant.

Note 2   *ff* instead of *f* initially is normal in the 15th century in place of the capital letter; it also occurs medially in many MSS even when no geminate is present.

How far initial *þ* in unstressed words, such as *thou* and *that*, was already voiced in ME cannot be determined from spelling.

Medially between vowels and between a vowel and a voiced consonant, *f* and *þ* had been voiced already in OE, although this could not be expressed in writing then; in ME spelling the introduction of the letter *v* or *u* clearly indicates the voicing of *f*, but that of *þ* remains unexpressed for lack of a distinctive letter.

Note 3   In the North, as a result of the early loss of final *-e*, *v* at the end of a word became voiceless, hence N *luf* 'love', *drif* 'to drive', *haf* 'I have'. Variations were produced by levelling with forms ending in *e* and a consonant (*-es*, *-ed*), so that *f*-spellings also occur in inflected forms, such as *giffis* 'he gives', *lyffed* 'he lived'. In the South *v* remained voiced even after the loss of final *-e*.

Before a directly following non-syllabic *m, n, r* or *l* there was a change of *þ* to *d*, as in ME *fadme* from OE (infl.) *fæðme* 'fathom', ME *birden, burden* from OE (infl.) *byrðne* 'burden' (beside *burþen* and *birþen* from the uninflected forms), ME *murdre(n)* from OE *morþrian* 'to murder'. Here and there *rd* also appears for *rð* in other positions.

From the 13th century, *v* before a consonant was often lost, sometimes by vocalising to *u*, hence *sen* for *seven*, *lady* for older *lavdie, larke* for OE *laferce* 'lark', but *hauk* for OE *hafoc* from the inflected and syncopated forms.

Finally, *f* and *þ* were voiceless only in OE, and remain so in ME.

Note 4 It is doubtful whether -*þ* in ME *feiþ* reproduces OF *đ* from Lat. intervocalic *d*, as *fei* also occurs in ME, and rather more commonly than *feiþ* in the earlier texts. Another possibility is an analogical introduction here of the Gmc abstract suffix -*þ*, as in *strengþ, trouþ, wraþ*, and *wroþ*, although the form *cariteþ*, found in Orrm and a few other eME instances, shows that the spirant (still often spelt *d* in AN; later lost in French) was taken over into English sometimes at least.

Note 5 *ʒ, z* or *d* for *þ* are errors by AN scribes, cf. §5, n. 2; *d* for *þ* (probably voiced) also occurs in 15th century MSS.

§37 Sibilants

A. OE *s*

OE *s* (uniformly spelt *s*) was voiceless initially and finally, medially it was voiced before and after voiced consonants and between vowels, and voiceless before voiceless consonants. In ME the quality was as in OE, except that in the South initial *s* became voiced (as did *f* and *þ*, see §36 above), although this is definitely indicated only in Kentish documents by the spelling *z*, as in *zelf* 'self', *zuyn* 'swine', *zuord* 'sword' and *zorʒe* 'sorrow'. Otherwise the usual ME spelling is *s* for both the voiced and voiceless sounds, save that occasionally *c* is introduced for the latter before *e* or *i*.

Note 1 Initial *st* remains even in the South, hence Kentish *sterue* 'to die', etc.

Finally, in unstressed syllables and words, -*s* became voiced in the course of the ME period, as is shown by the spelling -*z* in some MSS, e.g. *findez* 'he finds', *þingez* 'things'.

B. French *s*

French *s* in loanwords retained the French quality, but note
that:

1. for CF [s] from Lat. *ce, ci, ti*, NF had [tš], spelt *ch*. Some
loanwords in English have the NF value, such as *chisel, chesel*
chisel, *launchen* 'to thrust', *cacchen* 'to catch', and others the
CF, as in *citee* 'city', *civil, certain, cercle* 'circle', *ceese(n)* 'to
cease' and *chacen* 'to chase'.

2. for CF *-iss* in the Lat. inchoative suffix *-iscis, -iscit* NF had
iš], hence ME *finish, punishe(n)*; similarly for Lat. *-sti-* in ME
ussher (Fr. *huissier*, Lat. **ustiarius* for *ostiarius*), *frusshe(n)* 'to
brush', and for Lat. *-xi-* in *isshe(n)* 'to go out' (Lat. *exire*).

3. French medial *s* in English borrowings remained before *t*
and *p*, but was lost before *n, m, l*, except that before *l* and *n* the
AN development of *s* to *d* is also found. Hence ME *haste, feste*,
cost, spouse, but *ile* 'island', *dine(n)* 'to dine', *painim* 'land of
the pagans', *male, fraine* 'ash-tree', and *idle* 'island', *didne(n)*
'to dine', and *medle(n)* 'to meddle' (OF *mesler*).

§38   Palatal and Velar Stops and Spirants

In OE the Anglo-Frisian separation of the original guttural
stops and spirants into palatal and velar is evidenced only in
the effects on neighbouring vowels and not in spelling; in ME
it appears both in the development of the consonants themselves and in their written representation.

The separation is particularly noticeable where the voiceless
stop *k* and the voiced stop and spirant *g* and [ʒ]—in OE spelt *g*
invariably, and when doubled mostly *cg*—are concerned; less so
with the voiceless spirant [χ], spelt *h* in OE, because this had
become a pure aspirate early in OE when initial, and when
medial had been lost between and before vowels; wherever it
remained, its pronunciation was governed by the preceding
vowel, and changes in the OE vowels produced variations.

The voiceless stop was palatal in OE before all original front
vowels (i.e. OE *æ* from Gmc *a*; *e* and *i* and the diphthongs derived from them: *ea, eo*, and *io*; *ǣ* or *ē* from WGmc *ā*; *ē, ī*, and
the diphthongs *ēa, ēo*, and *īo*); medially, though, only before
Gmc *i* or *j* (even when these had been changed or lost in OE)
and after *ĭ* before front vowels; and finally only after *ĭ*. (Medially, loss of palatalisation is also probable when palatal [k′] came

to stand before consonants as a result either of the loss of *j* before
a back vowel in inflexions or of the syncope of a previous *i*; some
ME instances without palatalisation can only be explained on
this assumption.)

But in all other positions the OE voiceless stop was velar,
i.e. (i) before consonants; (ii) before back vowels; (iii) before
ǣ derived from *ă*, *ē* from *ō*, and *ȳ* from *ŭ* by *i*-mutation;
(iv) before OE *a* in open syllables when there is a back vowel
in the next syllable; and (v) before OE *a* followed by *ll*, *rr*, and
l or *r* plus a consonant (i.e. in those positions where otherwise
breaking produces *ea*).

A voiced stop occurred initially in OE only before original
back vowels (*ă*, *ŏ*, *ŭ* and their *i*-mutation results *ǽ*, *ĕ*, *ȳ*) and
before consonants; medially and finally only in the group *ng*,
and in geminates. In all these positions it was velar (guttural),
except that medially before an original *j* or *i* it became palatal
and remained so even when the *j* or *i* was lost in OE.

Old English had a spirant in all other positions, i.e. everywhere medially and finally except in the group *ng* and in
geminates, and initially before all original front vowels.

This spirant was a palatal [j] when initial, when medial between front vowels, and when final after front vowels. It was
velar, on the other hand, between and before back vowels medially, and after back vowels finally, provided that it had not
been levelled out to the voiceless [χ] of the inflected forms.

During the OE period and the transition to ME, this voiced
velar spirant became palatal, however, whenever back vowels
were fronted as a result of sound changes (e.g. when *ēa* or *ēo* was
smoothed to *ē*, or when back vowels in endings were weakened
to [ə]).

1. THE VOICELESS STOP

The voiceless velar stop, usually spelt *c* in OE, remains in ME.
The usual spelling is *c* before *a*, *o*, and *u*; *k* before *e*, *i* and *y*;
k or *c* before consonants; and *c*, *k*, or *ck* finally. Examples are.
ME *kai* 'key' (OE *cǣg*, with *ǣ* as the *i*-mutation of *ā*, Gmc *ai*);
cussen or *kisse(n)* 'to kiss' (OE *cyssan*); *knight*; *cloth*, N *clath*
'cloth'; *cow*; *cold*, N *cald* 'cold' (beside Kt *chald*, *cheald* from WS,
Kt *ćeald*); *make(n)* (OE *macian*); *speke(n)* 'to speak' (OE *sprecan*);
book; and *black*.

The voiceless palatal stop, also spelt *c* in OE, has the sound
tš] in ME, spelt *ch* or *cch*. The regular development is some-
imes disturbed by levelling between inflexions which had either
‹ velar or a palatal sound after the vowel, by the adoption of
Ꞩorse loanwords, and by partial assimilation of English words
‹o Norse phonology. Hence ME *chin*; *chirche* 'church' (OE *ċyrċe*
vith later rounding of *i*) beside *kirk* (from Norse); *chele* 'cold'
with *e* from *æ* by *i*-mutation); *chary* (OE *ċæriġ*, *ċeariġ*) beside
are 'care' (OE *caru*); *chep* 'bargain' (with *ēa* in OE); *biseech*
beseech' (OE *besēċan*, weak 1, and so with Gmc *j*) beside *seek*
lue to levelling out between inflected forms; similarly *dich* 'ditch'
)eside *dike* (OE *dīċ*); *birch* (OE *bierċe*, *birċe*) beside *birk* (from
Ꞩorse); and *ich* 'I' beside *ik* (by analogy with ON *ek*).

The OE group [sk] is [š] in ME, spelt *sch*, *sh*, (sometimes also
•*s* or *s*, initially also *x*, medially and finally also *ssch* or *ssh*), in
:ertain positions, viz. initially before all vowels, medially except
)efore back vowels, and finally except after back vowels—save
hat in the WS area and to some extent in the Kentish, meta-
hesis to [ks], spelt *x*, occurred, initially before and finally after,
▸ack vowels. Hence ME *scharp*, *schip*, *scho* 'shoe', *fressch*
fresh', *wassche(n)* 'to wash', but *ask* beside S *axe(n)* 'to ask',
usk, *duske(n)* 'to grow dark'.

The group [skr] remained initially in the South West, North
West Midlands and North; elsewhere (particularly in the East)
t became [šr], spelt *schr* or *shr*. Hence ME *scrappe(n)* beside
•*chrape(n)* 'to scrape', *skreme* beside *schreme(n)* 'to scream', and
•*crewe* beside *shrewe* 'shrew'.

Otherwise *sk* occurs in ME only in Norse, French, Latin and
Ɔutch borrowings, such as *sky*, *skin* and *skirte* (from Norse);
:*carce*, *scorn* and *escape(n)* (from French); *school* (from Latin);
ɪnd *skipper* and *scoure(n)* 'to scour' (from Dutch).

Note 1 In the North [š] in the post-tonic syllable [iš] became *s*,
ɪence *inglis* 'English', *perisse* 'to perish', *punnys* 'to punish'. Other
ɪnstances of *s* for [š] in the North are in the suffix *-ship*, as in *worsip*
'worship' and *felawsip* 'fellowship', and in the auxiliary verb *sal* 'shall'
ɪnd *sulde* 'should'.

French *k* (before *o* or *u*) was adopted unchanged; moreover
ꞨF had *k* before Lat. *a* (retained, or changed into *é* in open
ꞩyllables and *e* in suffixes) where CF had [tš], spelt *ch*. Some
)orrowings in English have the NF form, e.g. *cacche(n)* 'to catch'

D

(Fr *chasser*, as in ME *chace(n)* 'to chase'), *carre* 'wagon', or *car-*
penter, and others the CF form, e.g. *cheef* 'chief', *chaumbre* 'room'
and *chair*. On NF [tš] for CF *s* before *e* and *i*, cf. §37.

2. THE VOICED STOP

The guttural (originally velar) stop is retained in ME, spelt *g*,
as in *god* 'God', *good*, *goos* 'goose' (pl. *gees*), *gilt* or *gult* 'guilt',
glad, *gripe(n)* 'to grip', *finger*, *dog(ge)* (OE *dogga*), and *frog(ge)*
(OE *frogga*).

Note 2   The voiceless stop sometimes appears instead of the voiced
finally, and medially before voiceless consonants in the group *ng*, as in
rimes like *nothing* : *drink*, and spellings like *strencþ* and *lencþ*. Otherwise
ng probably became a guttural nasal [ŋ] in ME before consonants and
finally (cf. §34, n. 1), and perhaps dental [n] after *i* in some instances.

The palatal stop is [dž] in ME, spelt *gg*, later *dg*, and also
after *n*. Hence *rugge*, *rigge*, *ridge* 'ridge', *egge* or *edge* 'edge',
seggen 'to say', *leggen* 'to lay', *sengen* or *singen* 'to singe' (cf.
§11, n. 16), *henge* or *hinge* 'hinge'.

Note 3   Forms with *g* instead of [dž], unless influenced by Norse,
arise from the generalising of forms with back vowels in the inflectional
endings, see above.

In French borrowings *g* is adopted unchanged, as in *gouvern*
'to govern', *glorie* 'glory', *grace* and *figure*. NF *g* instead of
CF [dž] is uncommon in borrowings into English, but occurs in
gayl beside *jail* 'jail', *gailer* beside *jailer* 'jailer', and in *gardin*
'garden'. On Fr *g* from Gmc *w*, cf. §32.

OF [dž] was adopted unchanged, spelt *g* or *j*: *geste* 'story', *jo*
'joy', *journee* or *journeie* 'journey', *majestee*, *image*, *age*, *burgeis*
'citizen', *daunger* and *chaungen(n)* 'to change'. (The spelling
instead of *j* also occurs.)

3. THE VOICELESS SPIRANT

Initially, the voiceless spirant had become an aspirate already
in OE. Before consonants (*hr*, *hn*, *hl*), it had already been lost
in OE, except in Kentish, where it remained until the 14th century. Before vowels it remained in ME, and only in words with
weak sentence-stress are forms without *h* found, particularly in
it for *hit* 'it', less often in *is* for *his* 'his', and *ou* for *hou* 'how'.
On *hw* see §32.

Note 4 AN scribes often vary in their treatment of initial *h*, both omitting and inserting it incorrectly.

Medial *h* between vowels had already been dropped in pre-historic OE. Before consonants (mainly in the group *ht*) and finally, the guttural spirant remains in ME, spelt *gh*, *ʒ*, less commonly *h*, and in the North also *ch*: hence *naught, laughter, broughte, rough, dough* and *high*. Its pronunciation was probably palatal after front vowels, velar after back.

Note 5 A gradual loss of [χ] is probably indicated by spellings, in Southern and Eastern MSS of the later 14th and 15th centuries, without *gh* or *ʒ* before *t* (*rite* for *right* or *riʒt*, *dowter* for *doughter* 'daughter', *brout* for *brought*) and in contemporary rimes of words in *-ight* (e.g. *right*) with those in *-īt* (e.g. *quite* 'to release'). There are also, in the 15th century, spellings with an unetymological *gh* or *ʒ* after *i* before *t*, as in *parfiʒt* 'perfect' (OF *parfit*). Even earlier, AN scribes exhibit various irregularities in the representation of the guttural spirant, which was foreign to them, such as *gʒ* or *th* for *ght*.

Isolated 15th century spellings attest a change of [χ] to *f*.

Note 6 Forms without final *-gh* derive from the inflected forms, as in *hie* for *high*.

In French words of Gmc origin initial *h* remains, as in *hardy, haste, hauberk, heron,* and *heraud* 'herald'. In Latin words *h* is sometimes but not always written, as in *houre* beside *oure* 'hour' and *ost* beside *host* 'host'.

4. THE VOICED SPIRANT

The voiced velar spirant when medial between vowels was vocalised in the course of the ME period to *w* and formed diphthongs with preceding vowels as described in §13B. Finally, it had been unvoiced already in OE. The unvoiced sound reappeared in ME in the North after the loss of final *-e*, as in N *dragh* beside S *drawe* 'to draw'.

Note 7 The Northern development of a voiceless spirant indicates that at the time of the loss of final *-e* the vocalisation to *w* had not yet taken place; the same conclusion is to be drawn from spellings in Orrm, who spells the voiced velar spirant as *ʒh*, e.g. *aʒhenn* 'own', *boʒhess* 'boughs', and also *eʒhe* 'eyes' (WS *ēage*; ME later *eie* or *ie*, cf. §13A.4, because the spirant became palatal after *e*).

Note 8 The evidence of the modern dialects suggests that in some instances the velar spirant developed into a stop, as in *drag*, which often occurs both in ME and in the 15th century, or in *hag* for *haw* 'hawthorn'.

It is doubtful whether spellings of *g* for the spirant which was origin
ally velar but became palatal under the influence of neighbouring sound
belong here—these occur in Western and South Western MSS of the
13th century, particularly in verbs belonging to the second weak clas
(-*ian* in OE, from -*ōjan*; and in the 2nd and 3rd person pres.ind.sg. -*ast*
-*aþ* in OE) derived from adjectives in -*ig*, such as *biblodegeþ* 'he bloodies'
sunegeþ 'he sins', and *weregeþ* 'he grows tired', and also in superlative
(OE -*ost*) such as *modgeste* 'most brave' (from OE *mōdig*), and in *witega*
'prophet' (OE *witega*). In these instances we may have simply spelling
of *g* for *ȝ*, which sometimes occur at this time.

The voiced palatal spirant remains in ME when initial, spel
ȝ and later also *y*, as in *ȝeuen* 'to give', *ȝelden* 'to requite', *ȝellou*
'yellow', *ȝerd* 'court', and *ȝesterday* 'yesterday'.

Note 9   The stop *g* instead of *ȝ* is found initially only in Norse loan
words or in words affected by analogy with them, e.g. *gete(n)*, *get* 'to get
(beside *forȝeten* 'to forget'), *giuen* in place of *ȝeuen* 'to give', *gest* 'guest'
or as a result of levelling, as in *beginnen*, which is modelled on the pret
and pret.ptc.

Medially and finally *ȝ* was vocalised to *i* and formed diph
thongs with preceding vowels; cf. §13A.

Note 10   Southern ME forms like *sede* 'said', *meden* 'maiden', and
ren 'rain' reflect the WS loss of *ġ* after front vowels before *d* and *n*.

III THE INFLEXIONS AND THEIR USE

PART 1 NOUNS

§ **39** Already in OE, to some extent even before the earliest
exts, the inflexions of the various declensions had been levelled,
•y the assimilation of smaller classes to larger. Thus, at the end
•f the OE period we find: (1) levelling of the stem-vowels in the
g. and pl. of strong *o*-nouns, where these differed, as in the late
)l. *hwæles* (beside *hwalas*) of *hwæl* 'whale'; and (2) extension of
he nom. and acc. pl. ending *-as* from masculines of the *o*-declen-
ion to those of other declensions (*i*-nouns, *u*-nouns with long
tem-syllables, and some nouns of minor groups: the *r*-, *þ*- and
•*d*- declensions).

In Northumbrian, moreover, the final *-n* of weak nouns had
nostly become silent; the genitive ending *-es* of strong masc.
nd neuter nouns had been extended to feminine nouns, and to
veak masc. and neuter nouns; and the pl. ending *-as* had been
xtended from the strong masculines to some neuter and femin
ne nouns.

Many other differences of inflexion between the various de-
lensions disappeared when all the unstressed vowels in endings
oalesced in a sound which was spelt variously at first, but later
ᵉ- (see § 24).

§ **40** Accordingly, the inflexions at the beginning of the ME
•eriod were as follows:

SINGULAR

om.:   no ending, or *-e*

cc.:   as the nom., or *-e* (feminines with long stem-vowel), *-en*
        (*n*-stems)

en.:   *-es*, *-e* (feminines), *-en* (*n*-stems), no ending (*r*-stems)

at.:   *-e*, *-en*, or no ending (with *i*-mutation)

PLURAL

om. acc.: *-es*, *-en*, *-e*, *-r*, no ending (with or without *i*-mutation)

en.:   *-e*, *-ene*

at.:   *-en* (from OE *-um*)

§41   Loss of Grammatical Gender

Further levelling of inflexions was hastened by the loss of grammatical gender. Levelling of forms which differed according to gender in the definite article (§56) and in the demonstrative pronouns (§57), together with the loss of the 'strong' adjective declension (§43) with its more sharply differentiated inflexions, restricted the means of indicating grammatical gender, and eventually the gender of nouns can be identified only by the personal and possessive pronouns used with them.

Variations of gender occur in many nouns already in OE, particularly late OE, and also in early ME; notably, nouns with nom.sg. in -e usually become feminine, those with nom.sg. ending in a consonant usually become masculine, and neuters whose nom. acc. pl. ends in -u usually become feminine. Variations are also produced by association of ideas (abstract nouns become feminine, because most abstracts already are), by transfer of the gender of native words to foreign words (Latin, French), and by the influence of natural gender (e.g. *wif* 'wife' changes from neuter to feminine).

The first clear signs of a complete loss of grammatical gender appear in 10th century Northumbrian. In Midland texts of the 12th century (e.g. Orrm) the position is already much the same as it is in Modern English, but in contemporary Southern texts (e.g. Laȝamon) grammatical gender is still quite well preserved and ceases to be so only in the 13th century. The old distinctions remain longest in the South East; not until the 13th century is their loss clearly indicated. Foreign, particularly Norse borrowings at first retain the gender they had in the language of origin.

After grammatical gender disappears, natural gender is usual in personal pronouns referring to nouns indicating human beings; the neuter pronoun is also used with the word *child* when the sex is not in question. The masculine pronoun is often used for the larger mammals, and the feminine is preferred for some birds (e.g. *nightingale*). In addition to the neuter pronoun, the feminine is used for placenames, as in Latin; *sonne* 'sun' usually —again as in Latin—has the masculine pronoun, while *mon* 'moon', *sterre* 'star' and the names of the stars have the feminine. *Deaþ* 'death' is personified as masculine, other abstracts

nouns (the virtues and vices, the sciences, *nature*) as feminine,
save that *Love* 'Eros' is personified as masculine, as in Latin.

§42 The Development of the Inflexions in ME

1. NOMINATIVE SINGULAR

In early Southern documents old masculines and neuters,
which had final *-e*, *-a* in OE, tend to end in a consonant, whereas
feminine nouns which ended in a consonant in OE often have
final *-e*. In the North final *-e* is already silent in the earliest ME
texts.

2. ACCUSATIVE SINGULAR

This was the same as the nom. in most declensions in OE;
where this was not so, nom. and acc. are soon levelled in ME.

3. GENITIVE SINGULAR

The *-es* ending of strong masculines and neuters becomes
general in all nouns; *-en* occurs only in some early Southern
texts. (The position of inflected genitives in front of the noun
qualified is already generally settled in ME.) The following also
occur:

A *Genitives Without Ending*

In these, vestiges of old genitives in *-e* (feminine nouns), *-en*
n-stems) and without ending (*r*-stems) may have been preserved, but in individual instances it is often not easy to deter-
mine whether the construction involved is that of a genitive
before a noun or that in which the uninflected genitive is used
as an adjective. Uninflected genitives of this sort are common
in later ME, especially in the North, e.g. *meidene croune*, *the*
wife rede, *his herte wille*, *his fader care*, *his moder absence*. In
nouns which end in *-s*, and before words with initial *s-*, uninflected genitives may also be for phonetic reasons, as in *Daryus*
ruster, *to paradise gate*, *hors feet*, *for Christ sake*, *my lady sister*,
but, in constructions like these, genitives in *-s* also often occur
even in the same MSS, as in *my ladyes sister*, *for Christes sake*.

B *The Construction with the Preposition* of

Apart from its local sense, *of* is used in OE to indicate the
material of which something is made (e.g. *he het getimbrian cyri-*

can of treowe 'he had a church built of wood'), and with partitive
meaning. In these there are points of contact with the use of
the genitive, and already at the end of the OE period the construction with *of* is common. In ME, as a result of the partitive
use, it is commonly used of things and ideas; with personal
names the inflected genitive is preferred.

C   *Possessive Dative with Post-posited Possessive Pronoun*

This construction already appears occasionally in OE, but
remains rare until the 15th century, when it first becomes commoner, e.g. in MSS of the *Canterbury Tales* in the titles *The Wy,
of Bathe hir tale*, *The Millere his tale*. Because of the phonetic
similarity with the inflected genitive, this construction is commoner in masculine nouns than feminine in most texts.

Note 1   Before the vowels of endings became silent, this construction and the inflected genitive *-es* differed (in masculine nouns) only
when written down: *his* as an enclitic lost its initial *h* and was often
spelt *is* (cf. §38.3), which left the division of words in writing as the only
difference.

4. DATIVE SINGULAR

Variations in the use of final *-e* occur earlier here than elsewhere.

In nouns with nom. and acc. sg. ending in a consonant, and
after prepositions especially, final *-e* is lost. As a result, there is
but one subject- and object-case in the sg.

In nouns with nom. and acc. sg. ending in a voiceless spirant
the dative often retains a voiced spirant before final *-e*: thus
nom. and acc. *wif* 'wife', but *to wyue*; nom. and acc. *lif* 'life'
but *yn his lyue*.

OE sg. datives with mutation are not retained; the stem
vowel is levelled out to that of the other sg. cases.

Instances of the dative in *-en* (in *n*-stems) occur only in very
early texts.

In OE the locative and—in nouns, but not in the strong adj.
declension and some pronouns—the instrumental had the same
form as the dative, but in such uses the simple dative was
already rare and constructions with prepositions were customary; in ME the latter only are employed.

Note 2 ME has one fossilised locative: *whilom* 'once' (OE *hwīlum*, dat.pl.), interpreted as an adverb.

Already in OE, then, the dative was mainly the case of the personal ('indirect') object. Occasionally, especially with verbs referring to written or spoken utterance, OE also used the construction with the preposition *to*, in order to make clear the object of the action. This construction is very common in ME, particularly in some authors. In the North and East *till* (ON *til*) is usual instead of *to*.

The position of the indirect object and of the construction with *to* (or *till*) in ME is not yet as fixed as in Modern English. In ME prose, where there are two noun objects, the indirect (personal) object (without *to*) precedes the direct object, and both come after the verb; but indirect objects, when pronouns, also often precede the verb; and constructions with *to* both precede the verb and follow the direct object.

5. NOMINATIVE AND ACCUSATIVE PLURAL

In the North and the Midlands the ending *-es* has already been extended to almost all nouns in the 12th century.

In the South East and Kent in the 13th century *-es* is the ending of most old masculines, and only a few *n*-stems keep *-en*. Both endings have been extended, in almost equal proportions, to the feminines and neuters, where *-es* prevails in the South East in the 13th century, but in Kent not until the beginning of the 14th.

In the South and South West in the 13th century *-es* has been transferred to some masculines and neuters, but masc. plurals in *-en* are found not only in *n*-stems but also in other declensions (except *o*-stems). Feminine and neuter nouns mostly keep the old inflexions, or form plurals in *-en* (even in French words, such as *chambren* and *joyen*), less commonly in *-es*. Only in the 14th century does *-es* prevail, and even then plurals in *-en* survive to quite a large extent.

Throughout England plurals in *-en* are usual in *oxen* and *eyen*, N *eghen*, *een* 'eyes'; common in *eren* 'ears' and *fon* 'foes'; occasional in *honden* 'hands' in the South, and in *schoon* 'shoes', particularly in the North, although this is also found alongside *schoes* in the South.

Mutation plurals still used in ModE are generally employed
in ME, which also had *kii* 'cows', and in the North *hend* 'hands'

Note 3 The distinction between the forms *wumman* or *wom(m)an*
for the sg. and *wim(m)en* for the pl. appears first in the South West and
then spreads elsewhere. Chaucer still has *women* for the pl. In the
North pl. *wemen* (with lengthening of *i* to *ẹ̄* in an open syllable, §12B)
also occurs.

The following *r*-plurals remain: *childer* 'children' (OE *ċildru*,
with a parasitic vowel after the loss of final -*e*, cf. §26), *lambre*,
lombre, lomber 'lambs', *calver* 'calves'. Sometimes, especially in
the North, -*en* also appears as well, as in *children, lambren, calv-
ren*, and almost invariably in *eiren* 'eggs'.

Uninflected plurals are retained:

A *In some old neuter nouns.* These are, particularly, names
of animals, such as *deer, hors, swin, sheep, neet* 'cattle', and also
þing 'things', *lond* 'lands' and in the North *werk* 'works'; but
plurals in -*es* also occur in these nouns (*þinges, londes, werkis*).
By analogy, originally masculine names of animals, such as *fish*
and *fowl*, are associated with those which were originally neuter
(but *fowles* is used when a number of individual birds is meant).

B *In French nouns.* In some French nouns whose stem ends
in -*s*, the French plural is adopted, as in *caas* 'cases' and *vers*
'verses'.

C *In expressions of measure after numerals.* In OE, most
nouns expressing measure had uninflected plurals or plurals in -*e*
and the ME forms may be reflexes of these, as in *pound* (neuter
in OE), *winter* in the sense of 'year' (an OE *u*-stem), *ȝeer* 'year'
(neuter in OE), *niht* (a cons.-stem in OE), *mile* (fem. in OE),
mark as a monetary unit (fem. in OE), and also by analogy
cubyte 'cubit'. On the other hand, numerals over 20 were also
used as nouns in OE, combined with the genitive of the expres-
sion of measure, and the ME forms may also be reflexes of OE
genitive plurals, as seems to be so in *foot* (nom. acc. pl. *feet*, but
OE gen. *fōta*) and probably in *fadme* 'fathom' (later *fadim* and
fathom with a parasitic vowel after the loss of final -*e*). And
again, expressions of measure can be taken as a unit, subject of
a singular verb—this is not uncommon in ME.

Note 4 Other instances of sg. verbs with pl. subjects are for different
reasons: (1) when the predicate precedes the subject, as in *That never was
herd so greet merveilles* (Chaucer); (2) when the subject is a pronoun,

especially in relative clauses in which the relative pronoun is identical in the sg. and pl., as in *all þe knyghtys þat þere was*; (3) when the verb agrees with the noun predicate instead of the subject, as in *And ye schul understonde that orisouns and prayeres is for to seyn a pitous wyl of herte* (Chaucer).

The converse, i.e. pl. verb with sg. subject, especially common in ModE with collective nouns, is still unusual in ME, which has e.g. *the peple fedden hem in greet reverence*, but cp. *And whan the lewed peple is doun yset* (Chaucer).

6. GENITIVE PLURAL

In early ME texts we find forms in *-e* (from OE *-a*), such as *kinge*, even in nouns whose nom. acc. pl. ends in *-es*; and also forms in *-ene*, such as *englene* and *kingene*, especially in Southern texts (this is a generalisation of the ending *-ena* of the OE *n*-stems). Later the genitive has the same form as the nom. and acc., but the construction with *of* is more commonly used in the pl. than in the sg.

7. DATIVE PLURAL

In early Southern texts the ending *-en* (also *-on*, *-un*, from OE *-um*, at the beginning of the period) occurs somewhat more often in the dative than in the nom. and acc., and even in later texts and in the North dative forms more commonly have *-e* or *-en* or no ending than do the nom. and acc.

Note 5 Stem-vowels which vary in the OE inflexions are often generalised: hence sg. *dai* 'day' (OE *dæġ*), pl. *daies* from the sg., or pl. *dawes* (OE *dagas*) and sg. *dawe* from the pl.; *stre* 'straw' (from the OE nom. sg. *strēa*) beside *straw* (from the OE gen. sg. *strawes*, dat. sg. *strawe*) and *strā*, *strǫ* (from Norse).

PART 2   ADJECTIVES, ADVERBS AND NUMERALS

Adjectives

§43   Inflexions

The distinction in usage between the strong and weak declensions of adjectives is not found in ME, even in the earliest texts.

In 12th century Southern texts, the strong declension still preserves a few especially distinctive endings, i.e. *-ne* (acc. sg. masc.), *-es* (gen. sg. masc. and neuter), *-re* (gen. and dat. sg. fem.), and *-re* (gen. pl.). Only vestiges of the weak declension remain: *-en* (OE *-an*) is found, especially when followed by a word with an initial consonant, but before vowels it often became -e.

As a result of the levelling of inflexions—both between the strong declension and the weak, and within the strong declension itself—the nom. sg. of adjectives (especially those applied to feminine nouns) has the ending -e, even when the OE form had no ending.

Often in OE predicative adjectives were uninflected; in ME they are invariably so.

In Eastern and Northern texts, as early as the 12th century, adjectives usually lack an ending in the sg., and in the pl. have -e in all cases (as long as -e remains). In later ME the inflexions are lost in the South too: the sg. has -e or no ending, the pl. -e; and after the loss of final -e (§ 27) all forms lack an ending, save that in the gen. pl. *aller*, *alder* remain when combined with superlatives, as in *allermost* and *allerbest*, until early in ModE.

Foreign adjectives follow these patterns too, and French plurals in -s survive only in stereotyped borrowed phrases such as *places delitables* and *lords spirituels*, or when predicative, as in *romances that ben royales*.

§44   Comparatives and Superlatives

The OE degrees of comparison generally remain in ME. In the comparative, when the application of the OE ending -ra produces a group of two consonants, a long stem-vowel is shortened (cf. §9); and after final -e is lost, a parasitic vowel develops from syllabic r (cf. §26), hence ME *greet*, cpv. *gretter*; *late*, *latter*. The short vowel is then transferred to the superlative, hence ME *grettest* and (with loss of t before s) *last*. Sometimes, though, a long vowel is restored in the comparative and superlative by analogy with the stem-vowel of the positive.

ME retains the following OE mutated comparatives and superlatives: *lenger*, *lengest* (from *long*, *lang*), *elder*, *eldest* (from *old*, *ald*), and *strenger*, *strengest* (from *strong*, *strang*), but forms without mutation modelled on the positive also occur.

Beside the comparative *māre*, *mǫre* 'more' (OE *māra*; cf. §11.4), the originally substantival and adverbial form *mā*, *mǫ* (OE *mā*) is used interchangeably in ME.

In the superlative (OE *mǣst*) the stem-vowel is mostly assimilated to that of the comparative: the usual ME forms are *māst* or *mǫst*, and *mę̄st* is less common.

§45 The periphrastic comparison using *mā, mọ, māre, mọre* and *māst, mọst*, has precedents in OE in the occasional use of *swiþor* or *bet* to express the comparative, *swiþost* or *betst* the superlative, particularly with participles and with groups of words, such as infinitives with *to*, whose meaning is equivalent to that of an adjective. These older methods of periphrasis are ousted, from about 1300, by those with *ma, mo, mare, more, mast* and *most*, which are used with both English and French adjectives, and with monosyllables and disyllables as often as with polysyllables. The preference for these, over comparisons indicated by inflexions, may in some instances be for metrical or stylistic reasons, but the fact that French did not employ inflexions to form comparatives and superlatives may have encouraged their wider use. The modern distinction in usage between the different forms of comparison is not yet discernible in ME.

§46 Adjectives as Nouns

Adjectives could be used as nouns much more in ME than in Modern English. In the singular, adjectives were used with the definite or indefinite article, with a possessive or demonstrative pronoun, to signify individuals, as in *þe blinde, þe lame, the hooli of god* (Wycliffite Bible, translating *Sanctus Dei*), and *I nevere saugh a more bountevous . . . n'a gladder . . . n'a more gracious* (Chaucer); and in the plural, with or without an article, to indicate groups of people, such as *þe innocent, þe riȝtful, lame and blinde*. Beside these, both in sg. and pl., a common method of making the meaning clear is to use *man* or *men*, as in these phrases from the Wycliffite Bible: *mylde men* (Lat. *mites*), *merciull men* (Lat. *misericordes*), and *the pore men in spirit* (Lat. *pauperes spiritu*).

Adjectives are rarely used without a following noun when referring to objects or abstract ideas, and are usually followed by *þing* or *thinges*, as in the phrases in the Wycliffite Bible, *Osanna in hiȝest thingis* (Lat. *hosanna in excelsis*) and *al thing that* (Lat. *omne quod*).

Adjectives which are often used substantivally are sometimes formally interpreted as nouns, and then have the plural ending of nouns, as in *þe poueren* 'the poor' and *alle quikes* 'all the living'.

On adjectives used as nouns with *one*, cf. §61.

Adverbs

§47   Adverbs from Adjectives

In ME, adverbs are still usually formed from adjectives by adding -e, and there is also the method of formation (found here and there in OE) which uses the suffix -*liċe*, ME -*liche*, Northern -*lik* (from ON -*likr*), and (at first in the East Midlands) -*ly* (from ON -*ligr*, -*liga*); the last of these is already general in the 14th century, except in the South, where it appears in London (e.g. in Chaucer) only in the second half of the century.

Note   Another explanation of -*ly* is that it comes from -*liche* or -*li* respectively (analogously with *I* from *ich*) with loss of -*ch* finally in an unstressed syllable—cf. §51.

Wherever OE had an adverb without mutation alongside a mutated adjective (as in *softe* adv. 'softly' beside *sefte* adj., *swōt* adv. 'sweetly' beside *swēte* adj.), levelling took place in ME; sometimes, as a result, both forms are used both as adverb and adjective: e.g. ME *swete*, less commonly *swote* (and *sōte*, cf. §32.1)

In OE certain comparative adverbs were formed with mutation but no distinctive inflexion; of these, ME retains *leng* 'longer' (beside the new formations *langer* and *longer*) and *er* 'earlier' and of other uninflected comparative adverbs, ME keeps *ma* *mo* 'more' and *bet* 'better'.

§48

There are some common adverbs consisting of inflected forms of nouns and adjectives used independently, such as the genitives *anes*, *ones* 'once' and analogically *twies*, *thries*, and *nedes* '(must) needs', and datives like *whilom* 'once'.

Note   *For þen ones* is written *for þe nones*, with a false separation of the *n*, as if *nones* were a noun; it is used in the sense 'for the moment provisionally'.

Numerals

§49   Cardinal Numbers

The ME forms are:

1   early ME and N *ān*, *āne*, and also *ain* in the North (cf. §5, n. 5); S *ǭn*, *ǭne* (cf. §11.4), and *o*, *oo* before words beginning with a consonant. As the indefinite article, shortened forms are used: *an*, before words beginning with a consonant *a*, and in the South sometimes *on* or *o* as well.

Note 1 The earliest Southern texts still have inflected forms: in the acc., *anne, enne* (masc.; OE *ǣnne*); in the gen., *anes* (masc. and neuter), *anre* (fem.); and in the dat., *anen* (masc. and neuter), *are, ore* (fem.; OE *ānre*).

Note 2 In 15th century South Western texts *won* and *wone*, with initial *w-* inserted (cf. §13D.2), also occur.

Note 3 On *an, one* as an indefinite pronoun, cf. §61.

2 Midland and Southern *tweien, tweyn, tweie, twei*, Northern *tway, twai* (from OE *twēgen*; *ei* and *ai* as in §13A.2, since the stem-vowel has been shortened, as Orrm's *twezzen* shows); eME *twā* (N also *twai*, cf. §5, n. 5), S *twō* (OE *twā*). The two forms are no longer distinguished in gender in ME, and are used interchangeably throughout the period.

Note 4 In early Southern texts there are some inflected forms: gen. *tweire*, dat. *twam, twom* (with the vowel of the nom. and acc., instead of OE *twǣm*).

Beside *bā, bǫ* (OE *bā*) and *beie* (OE *bēgen*) 'both' *bāþe, bǫþe* (from ON *báþir* or OE *bā þā*) also exist.

Note 5 Inflected forms in early texts are gen. *beire, baþre* and dat. *boþen.*

3 *þreo* (*þro, þru*, §10), *þree* (OE *þrēo*, fem. and neuter); and in Southern texts also *þri, þrie* (OE *þrī, þrie*, masc.).

Note 6 In early Southern texts we also find dat. *þreom, þrem.*

4 *feower, feor*, more commonly *fower, four* (with [ou] or [ū], cf. §13, n. 6), inflected *foure*. Otherwise we have *faur* (cf. §13, n. 7) and Southern *vower, voure* (cf. §36).

5 *fif*, inflected *five*, in the South also *vif, vive* (§36).

6 *sex, six*, inflected *sixe, sexe.*

7 *seouen, seuen*, inflected *seouene, seuene.*

8 *ehte, eight(e)*, Orrm *ehhte*, and in the North *acht, aght, aught* (cf. §13C.1 and n. 10, n. 12).

9 *niȝen, niȝe*, later *nin(e)* (§13A.5), N *nēȝen, neen* (with *i* lengthened to *ē*, §13, n. 4), Kentish *neoȝen* (from OE **niogon, neogon* with back mutation).

10 *teon, teen, ten*, inflected *teene, tene.*

11 *endleue(ne), enleue(ne), elleue(ne).*

12 *twelf*, inflected *twelue*; in the South West *tweolf, tweolue* from Mcn *twœlf* with rounding of *-e-* after *w-*.

13 *þreoten(e), þretten(e), þritten(e).*

14-19 are formed from the words for 4-9 and the suffix *-ten(e).*

Note 7   The inflected (plural) forms are used when the numbers
stand alone; both the inflected and uninflected forms are found attribu
tively. After the loss of final -*e*, forms with a voiced spirant continue to
be used indifferently alongside those with a voiceless spirant.

20   *twenti*.

30   *þritti, þretti, thirti*.

40   *feowerti, fowerti, feorti, fourti*.

50   *fifti*.

60   *sexti, sixti*; also *three score*.

70   *seoventi, seventi*; in early texts *hundseventi*.

80   *eiȝteti, eiȝti*. The expected N form with *a, au* is not
attested, and from quite early *fourscore* is used instead.

90   *niȝenti, ninti*.

100   *hundred, hundrid, hondred, hunderd, hundurd*; and (from
ON *hundrað*) *hundreþ*. Only in early texts and in compounds
such as *hundfald* 'a hundredfold' is *hund* found.

1000   *þousend, þousind, þousand, þousond*.

1,000,000   *millioun*.

Note 8   Smaller numbers combined with larger, by means of *and*
can either precede or follow them.

§50   Ordinal Numbers

In OE the ordinals, except *oþer*, were declined as weak adjectives; in ME they have final -*e*, as long as it remains (§27); in
addition to the forms with the ending cited below there are,
accordingly, later ones without it.

1st   *furste, firste*; Kentish *uerste* (cf. §11.5 and §36); in the
South East (and in other areas, §11, n. 16) *ferste*; in the 15th
century also *frist*. Only infrequently does *forme* occur; *formes*
is also found (and also the comparative *former*).

2nd   *oþer*; and (from the second half of the 14th century)
secounde.

Note 1   In early Southern texts there are forms of *oþer* declined as
a strong adjective: in the singular, acc. *operne, opren* (masc.), gen. *opre*
(masc. and neuter); and in the plural, nom.acc. *opre*, gen. *opre*, dat.
opren, operen.

3rd *þrid(d)e*, *þrede*; *þirde*, and in the North also *þerd*.

4th *feorþe*, *ferþe*, Kentish *uerþe*; *fourþe* (modelled on *four*); *erde*, *firde*, *furde* (with *þ* becoming *d* as in §36; *i* from *e* as in 11, n. 16, and *u* for *eo* as in §10); *fourte* (with *t* on the model of *fte*).

5th *fifte*, later also *fifthe*.

6th *sexte*, *sixte*.

7th *seoveþe*, *seveþe*, *sefþe* (OE *seofoþa*); *sefte* (on the model of *fte*); *sevende* (Midland and Kentish; Angl. *seofunda*); *seovenþe*, *evenþe* (on the model of the cardinal); *sevente*.

8th *ehtuþe*, *eiȝtiþe*, *eighteþe* (OE *eahtoþa*, *ehtoþa*, *eahteþa*), and he syncopated forms of these, *eiȝtthe*, *eiȝt*; Northern *aȝtþe*, *aght*, ut normally *aghtand(e)*, *auchtande* from Norse **ahtande*; *ehh-:nnde* (in Orrm, probably modelled on *sevende*), *eghtende*.

9th *niȝeþe*, *nieþe* (OE *nigoþa*, *nigeþa*); *niȝhende*, Northern *eȝende* (modelled on the cardinal, as with *sevende*); *niend*, *nind* (ON *nionde*); *nineþe*, *ninþe*; *ninte* (modelled on the cardinal).

10th *teoþe*, *teþe* (OE *tēoþa*); *tenþe* (probably modelled on the ardinal); *tēnde* (probably from ON *tionde*).

11th *endlefte*, *ellefte* (OE *endlefta*, *ellefta*), less commonly *elle-ende*, *enlevenþ* (modelled on the cardinal).

12th *tweolfte*, *twelfte*.

13th-19th are formed from the cardinal numbers and the uffix *-teoþe*, *-teþe* (OE *tēoþa*), or the suffix *-tenþe*, *-tende*.

Numbers above 20th are formed from the cardinal and the uffix *-tiȝeþe*, *-tiȝþe*, *-tiþe*; in the South in the 14th and 15th enturies the suffix is *-tiest*.

The upper ordinals are rarely written out in full in MSS, but ndicated by Roman numerals, and in the 15th century by Arabic as well; sometimes, too, the cardinal is used.

Note 2 For the noun 'tithe' ME has *tiþe* (OE *tigoþa*).

PART 3   PRONOUNS

Personal and Possessive Pronouns

PERSONAL PRONOUNS

§51   First Person

SINGULAR

Nom.: *ich*; later *I* (from the 12th century, first before word
with an initial consonant, particularly [š] as in *ischall* for *ic*
schall; in the North *I* is from OE *ih* with *h* for *c* finally in a
unstressed word); in the North also *ik* (based on ON *ek*).
Obl.: *me*.[1]

PLURAL

Nom.: *we*.[1]
Obl.: *ous*; *us*.[2]

§52   Second Person

SINGULAR

Nom.: *þou*; also *þu*[2], and when enclitic *-te* (as in *wilte* 'wil
thou', *seiste* 'sayest thou').
Obl.: *þee*, shortened *þe*.

PLURAL

Nom.: *ȝee*, shortened *ȝe*.
Obl.: *eow, eu, iu* (from OE *ēow*); *ȝuw, ȝou* [jū] with stress-shif
and change of [ou] to [ū] (§13, n. 6); *ȝeu, ȝiu* as mixed forms
and *ȝe* as a reduced form in weakly stressed positions.

The nom. and obl. are still generally distinguished in ME.

The duals *wit* and *ȝit* still occur in the 13th century; later they
are given up and replaced by the plural.

From the 13th century, plural forms are found as polite form
of address.

---

[1] Long, or shortened when weakly stressed.
[2] Shortened when weakly stressed.

§53   Third Person

SINGULAR[1]

Masculine

Nom.: *he* (long, or shortened when weakly stressed); *ha, a*
when unstressed).

Acc.: *hine* (only in early Southern texts, and later replaced
by *him* as the oblique case).

Dat. (Obl.): *him*.

Feminine

Nom.: *heo*; in the West also *ho* and *hue* (from OE *hēo*, cf. §10);
later and Eastern *he* (unrounded, cf. §10); Kentish *hie* and *hi*
from OE *hēo*, cf. §11, n. 20). The unstressed forms are *ha* and *a*;
in the West Midlands there is *hoo*, which has [ū] in the modern
dialects (probably from OE *hēo* with stress-shift); in Orrm and
the South West *ȝho, ȝoo* (from OE *hēo* with stress-shift and *ȝ*
from pretonic *e*); in the East and South West *ȝe, ȝhe* (probably
a mixed form from *ȝho* and *he*). *Sche* appears first in the East
and from the 14th century also in London and the West; *scho*
is found in the North particularly, in the West occasionally.

Note 1   *Sche* and *scho* have not been satisfactorily explained. Their
origin has been thought to be the OE demonstrative *sēo*, from which
scho could be explained as deriving by stress-shift; but a development
from *ȝe, ȝo* after *s*, as in *was ȝe, is ȝe*, or after the Northern ending *-s* of
the 3rd pers.sg.pres.ind. (cf. §68), is possible, as is a development of *hj*
to [š], which did in fact occur in some placenames in the parts of
England occupied by the Norsemen.

Acc.: *hi*; *heo* (based on the nom.) only in early Southern texts,
and later replaced by the dative.

Dat.: *hire, heore, hure*; in the 14th and 15th century, especially
in the West, *her(e)*.

Neuter

Nom. and acc.: *hit* and (as in §38.3) *it*.

Note 2   No neuter dative forms are preserved.

---

[1] These forms originally refer to grammatical gender, but are later used
according to natural gender (cf. §41).

PLURAL

Nom.: the native forms are *heo, ho, he* (from OE *hēo*); *ha* i
weakly stressed positions; *hi* and *hie* (from OE *hī, hīe*), an
Western *huy* (OE *hȳ*). The form of Norse origin is *þei* (*þeȝȝ* i
Orrm), which appears first in the East Midlands and the North
from the 14th century also in the North West Midlands an
London. (It is from ON *þeir*, originally the demonstrative pro
noun, used instead of the 3rd person pronoun; as a demonstra
tive and relative, *þæȝe* occurs in South Western texts as earl
as the 11th century.)

Acc.: *heo, hi, hie*, weak-stressed *ha*; only in early texts, an
later replaced by the dative as the oblique case; in Kent *hi*
and in the East *hes*, which remain until the 14th century.

Dat. (Obl.): *heom, hom, hem* (OE *heom*); weak-stressed *ham*
him (OE *him*); *þeim* and *þaim* (from ON *þeim*; Orrm has *þeȝȝm*)
found at first in the East Midlands and North; *þem* in the East
Midlands from the 14th century, *þam* in the North. From th
15th century *þeim* and *þem* spread to London, but *hem* (which
predominates in the West to the end of the ME period) remain
as well.

Note 3 *þem* and *þam* are either weak-stressed forms of *þeim*, o
derive from the OE dem. *þǣm* (which could have remained in th
dialects even though 12th and 13th century examples of it are lacking)
The use of dem. forms instead of forms of the personal pronoun ca
be seen already in 10th century Northumbrian texts. The form *þer*
probably displaces *hem* because the nom. is *þey*.

POSSESSIVE PRONOUNS

§54   A   *Adjectival*

First Person: Singular *mīn*, and *mī* before a word with a
initial consonant; plural *our(e)*.

Second Person: Singular *þīn, þī* (as with *mīn*); plural *eower*
ower (OE *ēower*); *ȝūr* (with *ū*, as early as the 12th and 13th cen
turies, as in *ȝuw*, or modelled on *our*), *ȝour*.

Third Person: Singular: masc. *his*; fem. *hire* (OE *hire*), *heor*
and *hore* (with Western *o* for *eo*, §10), *here* (OE **heore*), weak
stressed *har*, and Western *hure* (from OE *heore* or *hyre*); neute
his.

Note 1   *its* as a possessive first appears at the end of the 16th century

Plural: *hire, heore, hore,* in the West also *hure* and in the South
West *hare* (Mcn *heara*), later *here* generally; *pair* (from ON *þeirra*),
at first in the East Midlands (Orrm has *þeȝȝr* beside *heore*); and
from the 14th century also *þer* (Northern) and *þar* (Northern
and Eastern). The forms in *þ-* spread to London in the 15th
century contemporaneously with *þeim* and *þem*, without com-
pletely displacing *her*; the latter remains in the West particu-
arly.

Note 2 *þer* and *þar* are to be explained as weak-stressed forms of
eir, or as from the OE dem. *þ̄ra*, although examples of the latter are
acking in the 12th and 13th centuries.

Adjectival possessive pronouns are declined as adjectives, and
o keep *-e* in the plural (similarly *his*, pl. *hise*).

B *Substantival*

ME has no substantival forms for possessive pronouns until
about 1300, when the practice begins in the North of adding
an *-s* (probably from the genitive) to *her, their, our* and *your*;
hese forms spread into the South during the 15th century.

§55 Reinforcement of Personal Pronouns; Reflexives

To reinforce personal pronouns (as well as nouns) OE em-
ploys the adjective *self, seolf*, WS and Anglian also *silf, sylf*;
likewise in ME, where the forms are *seolf, self, sulf, silf*, obl. and
pl. *selue, seluen*.

Originally, *self* was used with all the cases of the personal
pronoun, but in the course of ME it ceased to be used with the
nom. From the 13th century *self* is also treated as a noun, and
hen combined with the possessive pronoun (although only in
he first and second person), so that we have both *my self* and
ne self, þy self and *þe self, our selue(n)* and *us selue(n), your
elue(n)* and *you selue(n)*, but *him self, hire self, hem selue(n)*, and
hemselue(n) respectively. Combinations with the 3rd person
possessives (*hisself, theirselues*) do not appear until the end of
he 14th century.

As subject of a sentence, these forms can be used both to
reinforce a personal pronoun and by themselves, as in *ȝho wass
ire self . . . widdwe* (Orrm), *alse himself seiþ, Thou thi silf art a
pilgrim*, and *I wol myseluen gladly with yow ryde*; and in the 3rd

person also with nouns, as in *David hym silf seide in the Hool Goost.*

Until the 15th century, reinforced forms appear as reflexive chiefly for emphasis, as in *To sleen hym self* (C),[1] but probably also for rhythm, as in *What sholde he studie and make hymseluen wood* (C) or *maken hymseluen dronken* (C). Otherwise, the ordinary personal pronouns are used as reflexives throughout ME and they only become less common than the reinforced form towards the end of the 15th century.

To reinforce possessive pronouns, the adj. *aȝen, awen, owʒ* (OE *agen*) is used.

Demonstrative Pronouns

§56   The simple demonstrative (OE *sĕ, sēo, þæt*, pl. *þā*) was also used as a definite article in OE.

The initial *s-* of some forms had been levelled out to the initial *þ-* of the others by the end of the OE period, and *se, sẽ* occur in ME only in texts from the transition period.

Inflected forms[2] still appear in Southern and Western texts of the beginning of the 13th century; in the East and North already from 1150 and in the South from about 1250 the definite article is uniformly *þe* in the singular and often in the plural, although in the latter *þā, þǫ* still appear (and there are isolated instances of *þō* until the 15th century). The neuter nom. and acc. *þat* becomes generalised as the sg. demonstrative; as the pl., N *þaa* and S *þoo* remain to the end of the 15th century. In the North, from the 14th century, there also appears *þas*, a new formation probably derived from *þa* and the *-s* of noun plurals, while in the West Midlands an alternative pl. is *þeo* (beside *þo* which may, however, be only a spelling of *þeo*), probably a new formation based on the pl. personal pronoun *heo*. Not until the

---

[1] Citations from Chaucer will often be marked in this way.

[2]

	masc.	fem.	neuter
sg. nom.	þe	þeo	þat
acc.	þan, þane	—	þat
gen.	þes, þeos	þære, þere, þare	þes, þeos
dat.	þan, þane	þære, þere, þare	—
pl. nom.		þa	
acc.		þa	
gen.		þere	
dat.		þam	

nd of the 15th century does *those* appear in texts written in the
modern standard language, and then it gradually replaces *þo* as
he pl. The form *those* is hardly a reflex of the long lost pl. *þos*
·f the emphatic demonstrative (cf. §57), but rather a new for-
nation by analogy with the pl. of the emphatic demonstrative
·*ese*.

Note 1 Vestiges of the use of *þat* as a definite article remain to the
nd of the ME period in *at the ton ende* (from *at that on ende*), and *the
·ther* (from *that other*).

Note 2 After a dental, *þ-* in the article is often assimilated to *t-*. On
he loss of *-e* in the article, cf. §29A.

Note 3 The instrumental of the simple demonstrative, OE *þȳ*, re-
nains in *forþi* 'therefore' and in the weakened form *þe* before compara-
·ives in expressions such as *þe more, þe better, neuerþeles, napeles* (OE
·æfre þȳ læs*).

Note 4 In ME, particularly in poetry, there is a usage (different
·om that of ModE) in which the definite article is employed with per-
·onal names preceded by appellatives which denote a title, rank, or
·ffice, as in *the king Edward, þe quene Margarete*; but mostly the article
· lacking, as in ModE. It is also used occasionally with personal names
·o which a descriptive adjective is applied, as in *the old Nicholas*, and
·ith placenames derived from appellatives, such as *the Black Heath*. On
·he other hand, river-names still normally lack the article.

§ 57 The compound (emphatic) demonstrative pronoun (OE
·om.sg.masc. *þēs*, fem. *þēos*, neuter *þis*, nom.pl. *þās* etc.) still
·as some inflexions in ME at the beginning of the 13th century
·n Southern texts; these are (apart from the nom.sg.): acc.masc.
·*isne*; gen.masc. and neuter *þisses*; gen. and dat.fem. *þisre* and
·*isse*; nom. and acc.pl. *þās*, later *þǫs*.

In the East Midlands and the North the neuter nom. and acc.
·g. *þis* is used for all sg. cases, from the earliest ME texts. The
·l. is *þise* (from *þis* and the adjectival pl.-ending *-e*) or *þese* in
·he East Midlands; in the North it is rarely *þise* and mostly *þir*
·or *þire*), which soon becomes the only form; occasionally, too,
·he sg. *þis* is used as pl. In the West Midlands the pl. is at first
·*eos* (or *þeose* and *þuse*—the latter has *u* for *eo* as in §10), prob-
·bly modelled on the nom.sg.fem. or from the dat.pl. *þeossum*;
·ater the pl. is *þese*. In the South, after the loss of inflexions, the
·om.sg.masc. *þes* is used beside *þes* as the sg.; the pl. *þǫs* dis-
·ppears after the 13th century and is replaced by *þese*, which,
·s ModE *these*, ceases to alternate with *þise* in the 15th century
·nd becomes the only form used in Standard English.

Note 1   The origin of *þir* is obscure. Derivation from the ON den *þeir* is not very likely, not only for phonological reasons but because o the fact that *þeir* was used as a personal pronoun and gave English *þe* (cf. §53). Perhaps *þir* originates in *þe her* ('which here') or *þe þer* ('whic there').

Note 2   *þese* is derived from the OE nom.sg.masc. *þes*, and *þise* fro the nom. and acc. sg. neuter.

The usage of *þat, þa, þo, þas, those* and *þis, þes, þise, þese* (o *þir*) corresponds in general to modern usage.

§58   The rare OE demonstrative *ʒeon* 'yon' appears in Nor thern ME texts as *ʒon*, both by itself and after *þat*. In Souther texts its place is taken by *ʒonder* 'yonder', mostly used adverbi ally but also as a demonstrative adjective, as in *at ʒonder hill*

The OE weak adjective *ilca*, which indicates identity whe used with a demonstrative, has the form *ilke, ilche* in ME; thi is mostly joined to the article, as *thilke*, or used after *this*, a *this ilke*. Later, however, it is displaced by *same* (ON *samr* first in the North and East.

Relative and Interrogative Pronouns

§59   Relative Pronouns

The OE relative particle *þe* occurs in ME only in Souther texts of the 12th century, both by itself and in combinatio with the corresponding forms of the demonstrative, particularl *þat* (and also in the compound *þatte*, which is already found i OE).

From the 12th century, *þat* is an indeclinable relative used fo all cases and genders, even the plural. Prepositions governin the relative are accordingly treated as adverbial and place either before the verb of the relative clause or at its end; i later ME the former position becomes less common and th latter predominates.

GENERALISING RELATIVES

OE *swā* (simplified from the OE interrogatives *swā hwylċ* o *swā hwā*) occurs only in eME texts in the weakened form *se*.

ME *swilk, sich, swuch, such, soch* (OE *swylċ*, often precede by *eall, all*) no longer introduces the relative clause but is trans ferred to the principal clause. The relative clause is then intro duced by *alse, als, as* (OE *eall swā, all swā*), as in *Wiþþ all swilk rime alls iss sett* (Orrm) and *swiche godes as we sen*. Not unt late ME and early ModE is *as* used as a relative without a preceding *such*.

INTERROGATIVES AS RELATIVES

The use of interrogatives as relatives had already begun in OE in relative clauses which approximate to the object of an indirect question, as in *ic gemete . . . on me sylfum hwæt ic lecge on weofode þinre herunge* 'I find in myself what I lay on the altar in thy honour' (Ælfric). In ME the nom. of the interrogative pronoun (S *who*, N *wha*, *qua* and neuter *what*) does not occur in attributive relative clauses, but only in subject- and object-clauses, e.g. *who be greued in his goost, gouerne him better* and *what þow fyndest þere, slee it*. The genitive (S *whos*, N *whas*, *quas*) and the oblique (S *whom*, N *wham*, *quam*) do also occur in attributive clauses, e.g. *Crist whas moderr ʒho wass wurrþenn* 'Christ, whose mother she had become' (Orrm); *Frauncys Petrak . . . highte this clerk whos rethorike swete enlumyned all Ytaille* (C); *for if a preest be foul on whom we truste, no wonder is a lewed man to ruste* (C). From early ME, *which* (OE *hwilċ*, *hwylċ*, ME *whilch*, *whuch*, *which*, *quilk*) occurs as a relative, as in *foure gleedes han we whiche I shal devyse* (C). The modern distinction by which *which* refers only to things first develops during the ModE period, and in ME *which* applies quite ordinarily to people, as in *The knyght cam which men wenden had be deed* (C).

So-called 'amplifying' relative clauses (i.e. those which are only formally subordinate, because their meaning is independent and contributes a new idea) are introduced in ME by either *that* or *which* (and in the oblique case also by *whos* or *whom*), as in *The double sorwe of Troilus to tellen, that was the kyng Priamus sone of Troye* (C); *And smale foules maken melodye, that slepen al the nyght with open ye* (C); *his felawe, which that elder was than he, answeryde, Seing his frend in wo, whose hevinesse his herte slough* (C); *Lord, to whom fortune hath yeven victorie, . . . nat greveth us youre glorie* (C).

Relative clauses without any introductory pronoun are found in OE with the verb *hātan* and sometimes verbs of similar sense, if the relative pronoun would have been nominative; these clauses are accordingly associated with the subject of the principal clause. In ME clauses of this sort are found with other verbs too, as in *was neuer prince had more treie and tene* (Robert Mannyng, *Chronicle*), sometimes associated with elements of the

principal clause other than the subject, as in *at the firste look he*
on hir sette (C).

§60   Interrogative Pronouns

A   *The Substantival Interrogative*

The OE forms were (in the nom.) masc. and fem. *hwā*, neuter
hwæt; in ME they are as follows:

Nom.: masc. and fem. *whā*, later S *whō* (§11.4 and n. 11),
N *whā*, *quā*, *quhā* (§32); neuter *what*, N *quat*, *quhat* (also acc.).

Acc.: masc. fem. *hwan*, *hwon* only in early S texts, later replaced by the dative as the oblique; neuter as the nom. (see
above).

Gen.: *whǎs*, later S *whōs(e)*, N *quǎs* (OE *hwæs*, with the vowel
assimilated in ME to that of the masc. and fem. nom.).

Dat. (obl.): *whǎm*, later S *whōm*, N *quǎm* (again with the
vowel assimilated in ME to that of the masc. and fem. nom.).

The OE instrumental *hwȳ* is the interrogative adverb *why*
in ME.

Note   In early Kentish and West Midland texts, *whet* and *whes* (cf.
§11, n. 2) occur as nom. and acc. neuter and as genitive respectively.

Normally the masc. and fem. nom. is used for questions about
people, and the neuter for questions about things, but *hwæt*
occurs in OE with reference to people when the question is more
general. This usage persists into early ModE, but after the 14th
century *who*, *qua* is preferred for all questions about people.
The genitive was always applied to both people and things.

As a substantival pronoun, *what* is originally combined with
the genitive of a noun to ask a question about one thing out of
many, and hence about its kind. In later ME, however, *what* is
also used adjectivally, i.e. combined with a noun in the same
case, as in *And eek in what array that they were inne* (C).

B   *The OE Interrogative* hwilċ, hwylċ

The forms of this interrogative pronoun in ME are *whilche*,
whiche, in the West also *whulche*, *whuche*, in the North *whilk*,
quilk (influenced by ON *hvilíkr*). It is used adjectivally and
substantivally to ask a question about one thing or person
among several; the difference between it and *what* is clear in
Chaucer's line *And which they weren and of what degre*.

C   *The Disjunctive Interrogative*

The OE disjunctive interrogative pronoun *hwæþer, hweþer* has the forms *wheþer*, less often *whaþer*, later also *wheiþer* (influenced by *eiþer*, cf. §67) in ME, where it is used as a substantival and adjectival interrogative pronoun, as in *That wheiþer of yow bothe that hath myght . . . may . . . sleen his contrarie* (C); *now chese yourselven wheither that you liketh* (C); *Tyll the dome be gevyn of the whethur make that sche schal be (Seven Sages,* Southern version). This usage persists into the 17th century; since then *which* has been used in disjunctive questions, as it is, indeed, already in later ME.

The neuter form *whether*, also *wher(e)* in ME, becomes an interrogative adverb in direct or indirect disjunctive questions, as in *For wheither that he payde or took by taille, algate he wayted so in his achaat* (C), although the disjunctive sense of the question is not always retained: note *wher me was wo that is no questioun* (C).

Indefinite Pronouns

§61   Apart from its use as a numeral (§49.1), OE *ān*, ME (S) *oon, one,* (N) *aan, ain* (cf. §11.4) is used as an indefinite pronoun 'someone'. The adjectival use of this pronoun is not easy to distinguish from the use as an indefinite article—which it encouraged—as long as the stressed and unstressed forms do not clearly differ. In ME the indefinite article appears in the South as *o, on* (cf. §49.1), and in the North both forms have the same spelling, so that the indefinite pronoun is clearly present only before personal names, e.g. *Oon Maximus that was an officer* (C), and before participles, e.g. *we sayn oon castynge out feendis in thi name* (Wycliffite Bible; Lat. *vidimus quemdam . . . ejicientem*).

When employed substantivally, the word is always clearly a numeral ('one, not many') in OE, but in ME *oon* is also used to indicate an individual without describing him any more precisely, no comparison with 'many' being intended; examples are: *Ryght in the same vois and stevene that vseth oon I koude nevene* (C) and *It is a custom to zou that I delyuer oon to zou in pask* (Wycliffite Bible; Lat. *Est autem consuetudo vobis ut unum dimittam...*). In the sense of 'one', thus including the subject, *oon* is first used at the end of the ME period, as in *He herde a man say that one was surer in keping his tunge than . . .* (Earl Rivers, 1477), and

in ME the usual method of expressing this sense is still by means
of *man, men* (also, especially in the South, *me*, because the word
is unstressed) with a sg. or pl. verb: e.g. *Man schal not suffre his
wyf to roule aboute* (C); *Men shulde wedde aftir here estaat* (C);
icomen ich am þoruʒ a child man cleopiet Jesum (*Legend of the
Child Jesus*).

The word *oon* is common in ME after substantival adjectives
preceded by an indefinite article—as in *an uncouth one* (Mannyng), *a lusty oon* (C)—where it is, strictly, pleonastic but is
used in place of other nouns of general meaning such as *man*
and *thing* (cf. §46).

Note The development of this construction is not quite clear.
Frequently in OE poetry and sometimes in OE prose, *ān* or other numerals follow adjectives and nouns to emphasise the number: e.g. *Ic wāt
eardfæstne ānne standen* (in one of the Riddles), *modiǧe twēǧen* (*Battle of
Maldon*), *hit wæs gāst ān* (the *Dialogues* of St Gregory). Similarly in ME
we find *And þis was said by tyrand ain* (*Cursor Mundi*), *ʒho wass ædiʒ
wimmann an* (Orrm). This order is also found when nouns are put at the
beginning of the sentence for heavy emphasis, as in *Apostel was he siþen
an* (*Cursor Mundi*), and even when nouns are combined with an indefinite
article, as in *a wonder maister was he on* (Robert of Gloucester). In addition, we have the usage, already in OE, in which *ān* follows indefinite
adjectives, as in OE *æǧhwilc ān*, ME *swa mightful an* (*Cursor Mundi*).
Neither in OE nor ME were adjectives very commonly used as substan-
tives with the indefinite article: a noun like *man* or *thing* was usually
added; which is the reason that from the 14th century *oon* is more and
more used in place of these general nouns.

§62 ME *any, eny, oni* (OE *æniǧ*, assimilated to *maniǧ, moniǧ*
or to *ǫn* 'one', cf. §11, n. 9) indicates an indefinite unit among
several, i.e. 'any', as in *how may ony man entre in to the hous of a
stronge man* (Wycliffite Bible), or *as any swalwe chitteryng on a
berne* (C). In affirmative expressions it develops the meaning
'every', when one is taken as the representative of all, as in
She was . . . for any lord to leggen in his bedde (C). *Any* in the
sense of the French partitive article (e.g. *haue ye here eny mete?*)
first appears in early ModE.

§63 OE *sum*, ME *sum* or *som*, means 'a certain person or
thing' out of many. In ME the sg. is used substantivally only
in enumerations, e.g. *He moot be deed, som in his bed, som in the
depe see, som in the large feeld* (C), and otherwise the idiom is
some man, some thing; but the pl. occurs quite generally in substantival use, e.g. *somme woln ben armed* (C). Adjectivally, *som*

dentifies one person or thing among many, as in *som bettre man,
om swetnes.*

§64 OE *āwiht, ōwiht,* ME *oght, ought, aught* 'something' is
used as a noun, as in *So that I coude doon aught to youre plesaunce*
(C); as an adjective it occurs only in early ME, as in *ʒef he is
ʋurþful and aght man* (*The Owl and the Nightingale*). Adverbially
t means 'as far as', usually combined with the preposition *for*
n the phrase *for ought,* as in *For aught I woot he was of Derte-
nouthe* (C).

§65 OE *nān* 'none', ME *nān, nǫǫn,* adjectivally also *nā, nǫ*
(at first before words with initial consonant) displaces OE *nāwiht,
nōwiht* of similar meaning, which remains in ME only in the
neuter form *nought, noght, naught, not, nat* 'nothing'; hence *He
nolde slepe in noon hous* (C), *Ther nas no man nowhere so ver-
uous* (C).

Note 1 In ME, *nought, not, nat* are used more and more frequently
beside the simple negative *ne,* both in combination with it (i.e. as a
double negative), as in *Ne suffreth nat that men do you offence* (C), and
independently, as in *Al thogh I coude not make so well* (C).

Note 2 With *noon, no* in ME there coalesces the adverb *nǫ, nā* (OE
ne *ā, ne ō* 'not always'), which is to be distinguished from the interjection
nō, N *nā* (OE *nā*), N also *nay* (from ON *nei*) 'no'.

§66 OE *ǣghwylċ, ǣlċ,* ME *elch, ech* 'each' and intensified OE
ǣfre *ǣlċ,* ME *euerilch, euerich, euery* 'every' are used interchangeably, e.g. *heelynge euery languor and eche sekenesse* (Wycliffite
Bible). In substantival use, *ech* and *euery* are indeed possible,
but *oon* is usually added when the reference is to a person, *thing*
when it is to an object. Examples of independent use are *That
ech him loved that lokede on his face* (C), phrases with *ech of us,
ech of hem,* etc., and *To serve and plese euerich in that place* (C);
examples with *oon* are *We dronken and to reste wente echoon* (C)
and *So hadde I spoken with hem everychon* (C); and an example
with *thing* is *And everything com him to remembraunce* (C). In
this usage *echoon, everyoon* and *everything* come to be identical
in meaning with *all.*

§67 The forms for 'either' and 'neither' are used both substantivally and adverbially. These are: OE *ǣghwæþer, ǣʒþer,*
ME *aiþer, eiþer, eþer* and OE *āhwæþer, awþer,* ME *auþer,* meaning 'either'; OE *nōhwæþer, nāhwæþer,* ME *nauþer, nouþer,* mean-

ing 'neither'; together with forms produced by reciprocal level‐
ling, such as *neiþer*, *neþer* and *ouþer*.

Eventually a second member is added: *eiþer* is combined with
or or *oþer*; *neiþer* with *ne* or *nor*.

Examples are as follows: (substantival) *Of othres hond tha*
either deye sholde (C) and *Neither of us in love to hyndre other* (C)
(adverbial) *for she kan either synge or daunce* (C) and *ne yeve u*
neither mercy ne refuge (C).

In the expressions *on either side*, *on either ende*, *either* is used
as an adjective.

PART 4   VERBS

§68   Inflexions

PRESENT

Indicative

Singular: 1st person: -*e*, later uninflected after the loss of final
-*e*, §27); in Scotland occasionally -*s*.

2nd person: -*est*, -*st*, in the North -*es*, -*s*.

3rd person: -*eþ* in the South and Midlands; -*es*, -*s* in the North.

Plural: -*eþ* in the South; in the Midlands -*en*, also -*e* from the
14th century, and uninflected after the loss of final -*e*; in the
North -*es*, -*s*; and where the subject is a pronoun, especially
post-posited, -*e* and uninflected.

Note 1   In the 2nd person sg. the ending -*es*, -*s* is found already in
OE in Northumbrian; in ME it occurs in the North Midlands as well,
although alongside -*est*.

Note 2   In the 3rd person sg. the ending -*es*, -*s* is characteristic of
Northumbrian in OE. At the beginning of the 14th century it appears
also in the East Midlands (Lincolnshire) and in the East (Norfolk), and
then spreads to the South and West, reaching London in the 15th cen‐
tury. Throughout ME, however, -*eth*, -*th* remains predominant south of
a line running approximately from Norwich to Shrewsbury. The origin
of the ending -*es*, -*s* is disputed.

Note 3   Syncopated forms of the 2nd and 3rd persons sg., maintain‐
ing the OE syncope, are common in the South and also occur in the
Midlands. In the 3rd person forms, final -*þ* combines with the dental
consonant which ends the stem to form -*t*, sometimes -*d* (e.g. *sitt* 'he sits',
bitt 'he bites', *stont* 'he stands', *smyt* 'he hits', *rit* 'he rides', alongside
stond). The later syncope in inflexions (§28) which is general in ME is

nly rarely reflected in spelling. Syncope is uncommon in French verbs,
ut *attend*, for instance, is found, on the analogy of the OE syncopated
erbs.

Note 4   In the 2nd and 3rd persons sg. few forms in ME have *i*-
nutation, or -*i*- as against the -*e*- of the 1st person and the plural. In
outhern texts, though, *dest*, *dep* (from *don* 'to do') and *gest*, *gep* (from
on 'to go') occur here and there alongside *dost*, *dop*, and *gost*, *gop*. In
iue (or *giue*, §38, n. 9) the -*i*-, if it is not the result of the diphthong-
sation after a palatal which took place in the South in OE (§10, n. 1,
ara. 5), may have been transferred from the 2nd and 3rd persons sg. of
he pres. ind., or may be due to analogy with *ʒift* 'a gift'.

Note 5   In the plural the ending -*es* is Northumbrian in OE. In the
4th and 15th centuries it occurs in the North, and in the East and West
Iidlands alongside the characteristically Midland ending -*en*, which
lerives from the subjunctive. In the East -*en* is found as far south as
he Thames, in the West about as far south as the northern boundary of
Vorcestershire, but during the 14th century it spreads into the South
to some extent with loss of the -*n*, i.e. as -*e*, or uninflected in accordance
vith §27). Until Chaucer's time the usual ending in London was -*eth*,
ut he himself has mostly -*en* or -*e*. Where the subject is a pronoun,
specially a post-posited one, forms in -*e* or without ending are usual
hroughout England.

Note 6   On *i* (*y*) or *u* instead of *e* in the endings, see §24, n. 3.

Subjunctive (*Optative*)

Singular -*e*, later uninflected (§27); pl. -*en*, after the 14th cen-
ury endingless.

Imperative

Singular (2nd person) -*e* or uninflected (as in OE); pl. S -*ep*,
p; M -*en*, -*e*, uninflected; N -*es* as in the indicative.

Infinitive

In the South -*en*, -*n* (from OE -*an*) remains until the end of
he 14th century, and somewhat longer in monosyllabic forms
ben 'to be', *seen* 'to see', etc.). In the Midlands -*en*, -*n* dis-
ppears rather earlier. In the North the infinitive ending was
a already in OE, so that (in accordance with §27) infinitives
re uninflected in ME from the beginning of the period.

Note 7   Inflected infinitives in -*enne* (from OE -*anne*) occur only in
arly S texts.

Participle

The endings are S -*inde* (from OE -*ende*, §11, n. 16), M -*ende*
N -*and* (as already in class 2 weak verbs in some Northumbrian
texts in OE, either from a form without *i*-mutation, or based
on ON -*andi*).

The ending -*ing* first appears (beside -*inde*) in the South West
in the 14th century it is found also in London, Kent and gradually in the Midlands (beside -*ende*).

As a result, the participle coalesces with the verbal noun
(formed in OE with the suffix -*ung* or -*ing*) which had meanwhile come to be used as a gerund (cf. §80). In the North the
two forms (participle in -*and*, verbal noun and gerund in -*ing*)
are generally kept separate.

Note 8   Boundaries between -*inde*, -*ende* and -*and* cannot be sharply
drawn; in particular, -*ende* is found in border-areas alongside -*inde* and
-*and*. In the East -*inde* is found south of the Thames, in the West south
of the northern boundary of Worcestershire; -*and* comes as far south as
Norfolk in the East, and Staffordshire and Shropshire in the West, but
it is displaced by -*ing* much farther north than these limits. The separation of -*ing* and -*and* is most obvious in 15th century Scots.

Note 9   French participles in -*ant*, -*aunt* (cf. §22B) and sometimes
-*aund* occasionally occur (e.g. *plesaunt*, *repentaunt*), particularly in set
phrases (e.g. *table dormaunt*, *knight erraunt*), and are treated as adjectives, quite detached from the verb conjugation.

PRETERITE

Indicative

Singular: in the 1st and 3rd persons the -*e* of weak verbs is
lost (§27). In the 2nd person, the weak verb ending -*est* remains
in the South, but is replaced by -*es* north of Lincolnshire and
Shropshire approximately. During the 15th century -*est* gradually appears in strong verbs as well, in the South. On levelling
in the stem-vowels of strong verbs, cf. §69.

Plural: the ending -*n*, lost in the North already at the beginning of the ME period, mostly remains in the Midlands and
South to the end of the 14th century, particularly before word
beginning with a vowel.

Subjunctive (Optative)

In the singular the ending -*e* is lost in accordance with §27
in the plural the ending -*n* is lost as in the indicative.

Participle (in Strong Verbs)

In the South the ending *-en, -n* is preserved only in the earliest texts, and then lost. In the North the ending (unlike that of the infinitive or the pret. pl.) remains except when the stem ends in a nasal—hence *writen*, but *bund, bun* 'bound', *num* 'taken', *runne*—but even then it is often written, although ignored in rime, as in the rime of *bounden* 'bound' with *round*. In the Midlands the northern part associates itself with the North, the southern with the South, but Northern forms spread southwards, even as far as London in Chaucer's time.

The prefix (OE *ġe-*, ME *i-*) remains in the South and is lost in the North; and in border-areas forms are found with both *i-* and *-en*.

§69 The Stems of Strong Verbs

1. In the North the stem-vowel of the 2nd person sg. pret. ind. had already been levelled to that of the other sg. forms before the appearance of the first ME texts, as had that of the indic. and sjv. pret. pl. In the Midlands this levelling begins later, at first in the 2nd person sg. indic., and not in the pl. and sjv. until the 13th and 14th centuries; levelling in favour of the pret. pl. or the pret. ptc. also occurs in classes II-V. In the South, including London, the old differences are maintained into the 15th century even in the 2nd person sg. indic., but one does find a few levelled forms.

2. 'Grammatical Change' (Verner's Law) in the consonant at the end of the stem in the pret. pl. and pret. ptc. is to some extent preserved, to some extent levelled out in favour of the consonant in the present and the pret. sg. Examples are:

with *s* or *r*:
  cheosen, chesen 'to choose': pret. sg. *chees*; pret. pl. (S) *curen*, later *chosen*, (N) *chees*; pret. ptc. (S) *coren*, (N and later S) *chosen*
  freesen 'to freeze': pret. sg. *frees*; pret. ptc. *froren*, later *frosen*
  forleosen, forlesen 'to lose': pret. sg. *forlees*; pret. pl. *forlure(n)*, *forlore*; pret. ptc. *forlore(n)*, N also *forlosen*;

with *þ* or *d*:

> *seoþen, seeþen(n)* 'to boil': pret.sg. *seeþ*; pret.pl. *suden, sode*ᵣ
> beside *soþen*; pret.ptc. *soden, isode*; but cp. the following
>
> *liþen* 'to pass': pret.pl. and pret.ptc. *liþen* (beside weak form
> such as *liþde*)
>
> *scriþen* 'to move': pret.pl. and pret.ptc. *scriþen*
>
> *cweþen* 'to say': pret.sg. *quaþ, quoþ* beside *quod* (see n. 12)
> pret.pl. and pret.ptc. *cweþen* (only the pret.sg. remains i
> later ME);

with *h* or *ȝ*:

> *see(n)* 'to see': pret.sg. *seigh, saugh*; pret.pl. *seiȝen, siȝen*
> *sie(n), saȝen, sawe(n)*; pret.ptc. *iseie* (later replaced by *ise(n)*
> cf. n. 16)
>
> *flee(n)* 'to flee': pret.sg. *fleigh*; pret.pl. *fluȝen, flowen*; pret.ptc
> *floȝen, flowen*.

THE CLASSES OF STRONG VERBS

Class I

Ablaut-series: OE *ī*   —   *ā*   —   *i*   — *i*
           ME *ī* — N and eME *ā*, S *ǫ* — S *i*, N *ā*¹ — *i*

Thus: ME *driuen* 'to drive', pret.sg. *draaf, droof*, pret.pl
S *drive(n)*, N *draaf, draue*, pret.ptc. S *idriue*, N *driuen*.

Note 1   On *ai* for *ā* in the North, cf. §5, n. 5.

In the pret.ptc. forms also occur with *e* (that is, [ẹ̄] produced from
by lengthening in an open syllable, §12B), e.g. *dreuyn* 'driven', *wretyₙ*
'written'.

Note 2   On the model of class II, *stie(n)* 'to climb' (OE *stīgan*) ha
pret.sg. *steigh*, and sporadically pret.pl. *stuȝe* beside *stiȝe(n)* and pret
ptc. *istoȝe* beside *istie(n)*.

Note 3   *strive(n)* 'to strive' (OF *estriver*) is the only French verb t
have stem-forms as in this class: pret.sg. *straaf, stroof*, pret.pl. S *strive(n)*
pret.ptc. S *istrive*, N *striven*.

Class II

Ablaut-series: OE   *ēo*² — *ēa* — *u* — *o*
               ME   *ȩ̄*² —   *ę̄*   — *u, o* — *ǫ*

Thus: ME *clȩ̄uen* 'to cleave', pret.sg. *clę̄f*, pret.pl. *cluuen*, late
clouen, pret.ptc. S *icloue*, N *clouen*.

---

¹ modelled on the pret. sg.   ² *ū* in certain verbs.

Note 4 In the pret.pl., *o* is not always a spelling for *u* (§5B); sometimes it represents a transfer of the *ǫ* of the pret.ptc. (which is from
OE *o*, lengthened in an open syllable, §12A).

Note 5 The verb *fleien, flie(n)* 'to fly' (OE *flēogan*) has, alongside
leigh, a pret.sg. *flew* by analogy with the reduplicating verbs which have
u in the pret.pl. and pret.ptc. (e.g. *ibrowe* 'brewed', *iknowe* 'known').
The verb *leien, lie(n)* 'to tell lies' has weak *lied(e)* as well as the strong
forms: pret.sg. *leigh*, pret.pl. and pret.ptc. *lowen*.

Note 6 Alongside *schete(n)* 'to shoot' (OE *scēotan*) ME has, as a result
of stress-shift, *schote(n)*, for which weak forms of the pret. and the pret.
ptc. (*schotte, ischot*, with short vowel as in §70.1) are later formed.

Note 7 *bēde(n)* 'to command' (OE *bēodan*) is commonly confused
with *bidde(n)* 'to ask' and later replaced by it.

CLASS III

(*a*) Before a nasal:

Ablaut-series: OE and ME   *i — a(o) —   u   —   u*
      before *nd* and *mb*[1]   ME   *ī — ā, ǫ — ou*[ū]*— ou*[ū]

Thus: ME *drinke(n)*, pret.sg. *drank* (*dronk* in the West, §11.3),
pret.pl. *drunke(n)*, N *drank*, pret.ptc. *idrunke*, N *drunken*;

finde(n), pret.sg. S *fǫnd* (§11.4), later also *found* (modelled on
the pret.pl. and pret.ptc.), N *faand, fand* (also shortened, cf. §8)
and *found*, pret.pl. S *funde(n), founde*, pret.ptc. S *ifounde*, N
funden, found.

(*b*) Before *l* or *r* plus a consonant:

Ablaut-series: OE   *e(eo) — a(ea) — u — o*
      ME   *e —   a   — u — o*

Thus: ME *helpe(n)*, pret.sg. *halp*, pret.pl. S *hulpen*, later *holpen* (modelled on the pret.ptc.), N *halp*, pret.ptc. S *iholpe*, N
holpen;

kerve(n) 'to carve', pret.sg. *karf*, pret.pl. S *kurven*, later *cor-
ve(n)*, N *karf, karue*, pret.ptc. S *icorue*, N *coruen*.

Note 8 Particularly in later ME and in the North and East, forms
derived from ON *renna* or OE *rinnan* are commoner than those from
OE *iernan, eornan* 'to run', just as forms from ON *bresta* are commoner
than those from OE *berstan*.

(*c*) Before *ht*:

The ME forms of OE *feohtan, fehtan* 'to fight' are: pres. *fighte(n)*,
rarely *feighten*, pret.sg. *faught*, in the North also *faght*, pret.pl.
S *foughte(n)* (with [ū] or [ou] from the pret.ptc.), N *faught, faght*,
pret.ptc. *ifought, foghten*.

---

[1] in accordance with §8.

CLASS IV

(a) Beside *r* or *l*:

Ablaut-series: OE　*e* — *æ* — WS *ǣ*, nWS *ē* — *o*

　　　　　　　ME　*ę̄*[1] — *a* — 　　　 *ę̄*, 　　　 *ē* — *ǭ*[1]

As the vowel of the pret. sg. and pret. pl., in both the North and the South, ME also has *ā*, which is probably to be explained as a transfer of the vowel of the sg. lengthened in open syllables, §12A, in the inflected forms. Not until the 15th and 16th centuries is *ǭ*, transferred from the pret. ptc., found in the pret.

Thus: *bere(n)* 'to bear', pret. sg. *bar, baar*, pret. pl. *bere(n), bare(n)*, pret. ptc. *ibore, boren, born*;

stele(n) 'to steal', pret. sg. *stal, staal*, pret. pl. *steele(n), stale(n)*, pret. ptc. *istole, stolen*.

Note 9　Pret. sg. *boor*, pl. *booren*, found infrequently in the South, are probably by analogy with class VI (*swerien, sweren*).

Note 10　In the East Midlands *ā* in the pret. pl. could also be due to a regular phonetic development (§11.2), but forms with this vowel are quite common outside the 'East Saxon' area.

(b) Before a nasal:

Ablaut-series: OE　*i* — *a, ō*[2] — *ō* — *u*

　　　　　　　ME　*i* — *a, ō* — *ō* — *u*

Thus: ME *nime(n)* 'to take', pret. sg. *nam* beside *noom*, pret. pl. *noome(n)*, pret. ptc. *nume(n), nomen* (with *u* spelt *o*, §5.2), S *inome*;

cume(n), come(n) 'to come', pret. sg. *cam*, also *caam*, beside *coom*; pret. pl. *came(n)* beside *coome(n)*, pret. pl. *icume, icome, cumen, come*.

Note 11　In some early Southern texts *come(n)* has forms with *i* or *e* in the 2nd and 3rd persons pres. indic.; these derive from OE forms with *i*-mutation.

The pret. *cam, caam* derives from an unrecorded OE pret. sg. **cam* (analogical with *nam*).

CLASS V

Ablaut-series: OE　*e* — *æ* — WS *ǣ*, nWS *ē* — *e*

　　　　　　　ME　*ę̄*[3] — *a*[4] — 　　　 *ę̄*, 　　 *ē*[4] — *ę̄*[3]

---

[1] lengthened in an open syllable.
[2] as in the pl., on the analogy of class VI.
[3] lengthened in an open syllable.
[4] the pret. sg. and pret. pl. also have *ā*, as with class IV.

Thus: ME *ete(n)* 'to eat' (OE *etan*), pret.sg. *at* (by analogy with other verbs of this class) and *eet* ($\bar{e}$ and $\bar{e}$, from OE *æt* and *ēt*), pret.pl. *ete(n)*, *ate(n)*, pret.ptc. *eten*;

speke(n) 'to speak' (OE *sprecan*, *specan*), pret.sg. *spak*, *spaak*, pret.pl. *speken*, *spaken*, N *spak*, *spaak*, pret.ptc. *speken*, *ispeke*.

Note 12 Under the influence of class IV, *speke(n)*, *wreke(n)* 'to avenge', *trede(n)* 'to tread' and *weue(n)* 'to weave' form a pret.ptc. with *o*- from the 14th century, first in the East and later elsewhere too; hence *spoken*, *yspoke*; *wrokin*, *iwroke*; *troden*; and *woven*, *iwove*. In the pret.pl. *ọ* is found only rarely in ME (e.g. *spoken*, *troden*), and does not become more general as the pret. vowel until the 16th century.

The form *quoth* 'said' (OE *cwæð*) is probably due to weak stress; *quod*, which appears as well, most likely has -*d* by analogy with *said*.

Note 13 Already in eME *treden* and *weue(n)* also have weak forms: *redde* (Wyclif), *trededd* (Orrm), *weuyd*.

Note 14 On the present vowel of *ʒiue*, *ʒeue* 'to give' (OE *ġiefan*) see §10, n. 1, para. 5 and §68, n. 4; on its replacement by the ON borrowing *ʒiue* see §38, n. 9. The pret.ptc. is *ʒiuen* and *ʒeuen*, beside *goven* and *ʒouyn*. Even early in the period there are isolated instances of a pret.pl. *ʒoven*, *ʒovyn*.

Note 15 *gete(n)* 'to get' (ON *geta*, cf. §38, n. 9) has *goten* as pret.ptc. as early as the 13th century, but the common form is *gete(n)*.

Note 16 *see(n)* 'to see' has pret.sg. *seigh* and *saugh* (as in §13, n. 10), beside *sei*, *si* and *saw* from a pl. modelled on the sg.; another pret.sg., *sigh*, is a mixed form with the vowel of the pl.

The pret.pl. is *seʒen*, *seien*, *sie(n)* (from OE *sēgon*), and *sawe(n)*, N *saugh* modelled on the sg., S *seien*, *sayn* (from OE *sǣgon*).

In the pret.ptc., the early Southern form *iseie(n)* is later replaced by *see(n)*, *seen*, which is either from the OE adj. *ġesēne* or analogical to *ibe*, *een* 'been' and *ido*, *doon* 'done'.

Note 17 The sound [dž] in OE *liċġan* 'to lie', developed from the OE geminate, remains in the 1st person sg. pres.indic., the pres.pl.indic., in the pres.sjv., and in the infinitive (as ME *ligge*, *liggeþ*, *ligge(n)*) only in the South; in the North the corresponding forms are *lie*, *lies*, *lien*, which spread to the South in the 14th century and in the 15th have already displaced *ligge*. Cf. §70, n. 2, and the section on class 3.

Class VI

Ablaut-series: OE $a^1 - \bar{o} - \bar{o} - a$

ME $\bar{a}^2 - \bar{ọ} - \bar{ọ} - \bar{a}^2$

Thus: ME *fare(n)* 'to go', pret.sg. *for*, *foor*, pret.pl. *fore(n)*, pret.ptc. *ifare*, *faren*;

[1] *e* in *j*-stems, as a result of *i*-mutation.
[2] lengthened in an open syllable.

schake(*n*) 'to shake', pret.sg. *schook*, pret.pl. *schooke*(*n*), pret
ptc. *schaken*, *ischake*;

stand, *stonde*(*n*) 'to stand', pret.sg. *stood*, pret.pl. *stoode*(*n*)
pret.ptc. *standen*, *ystonde* (with lengthening before *nd*, §68).

Note 18   The forms of *take*(*n*) 'to take' (ON *taka*) follow this class
as in ON: pret. *took*, *toke*(*n*), pret.ptc. *taken*, *itake* and N *tan* (whence
the N present *ta*).

Note 19   The verb 'to slay' (OE *slēan*) in ME has, alongside th
infinitive *sle*(*n*), also *slā*, *slǭ* (from ON *slá*); and alongside the pret. *slogh*
slough, *slowe*(*n*) one finds *slew*, modelled on the reduplicating verbs.

Note 20   On the analogy of class IV, ME *swerie*(*n*), *swere*(*n*) 't
swear' has a pret.ptc. *iswore*, *sworen* and (in the North and East) a pret
swar, *swāre*; and ME *hebbe*(*n*) (OE *hebban*) has a pret. *haf*, *haaf* and
pret.ptc. *hofen*.

Note 21   *waxe*(*n*), *wexe*(*n*) 'to grow' (OE *weaxan*) and *wasche*(*n*) 't
wash' go over to the reduplicating verbs; *waxe*(*n*) thus has pret. *wẹẹ*
wẹẹxe(*n*), pret.ptc. *waxen*, *wexen*, beside forms proper to class IV: pret
wax, pret.ptc. *woxen*. The pret. of *wasche*(*n*) is *wẹsch*, the pret.pt
waschen.

Similarly, *hebbe*(*n*) has a pret. *hẹf*.

CLASS VII (REDUPLICATING VERBS)

These verbs had *ē* or *ēo* in the pret. in OE, *ẹ* or *eo* [ō], later
(§10) in ME, hence:

fōn 'to take', pret. *feeng*; the present later has *fange*(*n*), *fon*
ge(*n*) modelled on the pret.ptc.;

lepe(*n*) 'to leap', pret. *leop*, *lẹ̄p*;

hōn 'to hang', later *hang*, *hong* from the pret.ptc.; pret. *heeng*
lete(*n*) 'to let', pret. *lẹ̄t*;

slepe(*n*) 'to sleep' , pret. *slẹ̄p*;

falde(*n*), *folde*(*n*), *felde*(*n*) 'to fold' (OE *fealdan*, *faldan*, cf. §1
n. 1, para. 1, lengthened before *ld* as in §8); pret. *feeld*;

halde(*n*), *holde*(*n*), *helde*(*n*) 'to hold' (OE *healdan*, *haldan*, c
§10, n. 1, lengthened as in §8), pret. *heeld*, *huld* (with [ö] spelt
§10);

walke(*n*) 'to walk', pret. *wẹlk*;

bete(*n*) 'to beat', pret. *beot*, *beet*, *bẹ̄t*;

hewe(*n*) 'to hew', pret. *hẹw* (§13B.8);

blowe(*n*), *blawe*(*n*) 'to blow', pret. *blẹw*;

knowe(*n*), *knawe*(*n*) 'to know', pret. *knẹw*;

flowe(*n*) 'to flow', pret. *flẹw*.

Note 22 *falle(n)* 'to fall' has pret. *fel* and *fil* shortened before *ll* (as n §9, n.).

Note 23 A number of verbs have both strong and weak forms: *ang*, *hong*, following the transitive verb OE *hangian*, *hongian*; *lepe(n)*; *ete(n)*, which has *let*, *lat* in accordance with §9, n.; *slepe(n)*; *wepe(n)*; *ete(n)*, which has *bette*; and *flowe(n)*. In ME weak forms only are found of *drede(n)* 'to dread', viz. *drĕdde* and *drădde* as in §9, n.

Note 24 *lepe(n)* also has a pret. pl. *lopen* and pret. ptc. *ilope*, *lopen* following class II, and similarly *wepe(n)* has a pret. ptc. *wopen*. Weak forms are common in both verbs.

Note 25 OE *hātan* 'to command, promise', ME *hāte*, *hǫte(n)*, takes over from the former passive OE *hātte*, *-on* the sense 'to be named' and develops a new present *hēte(n)*, modelled on the pret. *hēt*, particularly with the meaning 'to promise'. The OE pret. *heht* remains in ME as *eight*, *hight*, interpreted as the preterite of a weak verb without connecting vowel (§70, Class 1 B); it accordingly often has a final *-e* and comes to be used beside *hāten*, *ihǫte* as a pret. ptc.

§70 The Stems of Weak Verbs

CLASS 1

A *With Connecting Vowel in Pret. and Ptc.*

In the preterite, already in OE, the medial vowel (i.e. the initial syllable of the ending *-ede*) had been lost in verbs with long stems and in verbs with short stems ending in *d*, *t* or *z*: hence OE *dǣlan*, pret. *dǣlde*; *dēman*, *dēmde*; *hreddan*, *hredde*; and *leċġan*, *leġde*. After voiceless consonants, *d* was unvoiced: *settan*, *sette*; *cyssan*, *cyste*; and *cēpan*, *cēpte*.

In the pret. participle, syncope occurred in OE only in the inflected forms of verbs with long stems, hence *hīeran*, pret. ptc. *ġehīered*, but acc. sg. masc. *gehīerdne*. In ME syncopated forms in the pret. are usually extended to the participle, hence *isett* 'seated', *ileid* 'laid' and *iherd* 'heard'.

In verbs whose stem has a long vowel followed by a consonant, the long vowel is shortened before the group of two consonants produced by syncope in the pret. and pret. ptc. (cf. §9.1): hence ME *kēpe(n)*, pret. and pret. ptc. *(i)kĕpt*; but in some verbs levelled forms with the long stem-vowel of the present are found.

On the eventual muting of the *-e-* in the ending *-ed*, see §28.

Note 1 In ME, *i* from [j] retained after *r* is preserved in the South and West into the 14th century; hence *werien* 'to guard', later *were(n)*, N *wer(e)*, and *herie(n)* 'to praise', N *her(e)*.

Note 2 In the inf., the 1st pers.sg. and the pl. of the pres.ind., and the sjv., ME [dž] from the OE geminate *ċġ* (§ 38.2) remains in the South into the 15th century, but in the North, usually in the Midlands, and from the 14th century gradually in the South, forms with diphthongs (§ 13A) modelled on the 2nd and 3rd pers.pres.ind. appear instead. Thus

OE *leċġan* 'to lay': S at first *legge(n)*, N, M and later S *lei(en)*;

OE *byċġan* 'to buy': SW at first *bugge(n)*, SM *bigge(n)*, Kt and F *begge(n)*, N *bie*, NW and later SW *bui(en)*, Kt *beien*, *baien*; and similarly the other forms. Cf. also § 69, n. 17, and the forms of class 3 weak verbs.

Note 3 In syncopated forms of the pret. and pret.ptc., *t* appears increasingly instead of *d* in ME, even after voiced consonants; this occurs first in verbs with *nd*, *ld* and *rd*, such as *sende(n)*, 'to send' *sente*, *sent*; *wenden* 'to go', *wente*, *went*; *gilden* 'to gild', *gilte*, *gilt*; later in verbs with a long stem-vowel before *m*, *n*, *l*, *r* or *v*, which is then shortened, such as *dẹle(n)* 'to divide', *delte*, *delt*; *dẹme(n)* 'to judge', *demte*, *demt* *lẹven* 'to leave', *lefte*, *left*; and in verbs with *nn* such as *brenne(n)* 'to burn', *brente*, *brent*. Sometimes *t* is extended to class 2 weak and French verbs, such as *clẹve(n)* 'to cleave (adhere)' (OE *cleofian*), *clefte*, *cleft*; *lọser* 'to lose' (OE *losian*), *loste*, *lost*; and *spoile(n)* 'to spoil' (OF *espoillier*) *spoilte*, *spoilt*.

This cannot be explained simply as unvoicing finally (§ 35) because it also, to some extent, affects previously inflected forms; analogy no doubt plays a part.

B   *Without Connecting Vowel in Pret. and Ptc.*

In these verbs the pret. and pret.ptc., besides lacking a connecting vowel in OE (as distinct from those in A above which lost it in ME), also lacked mutation.[1] The ME forms develop according to normal sound laws from those of OE; certain dialectal differences (before *ld*, § 10, n. 1, para. 1, and before *ht* § 13C) are to be noted.

Note 4   *quelle(n)* 'to kill' and *dwelle(n)* also have an analogical pret. and pret.ptc. based on the present: *quelde*, *dwelde*, and *dwelt* as in n. above.

CLASS 2

PRESENT

The *-i-* of the present stem has already been lost in the North and East in the earliest ME texts, but in the South and West it persists into the 14th century, so that the endings are: inf. *-ie(n)*, *-i(n)*; 1st pers.sg.ind. *-ie*, *-i*; ind.pl. *-ieþ*, *-iþ*; sjv. *-ie(n)* *-i(n)*; ptc. *-iende*, *-inde*. The *-i-* remains longest in the verbs *lou* 'to love' (OE *lufian*) and *wony* 'to dwell' (OE *wunian*).

[1] This absence of mutation is called 'Rückumlaut'.

Note 5 The original distinction between forms with *-ie-* and those with *-i-* (in the inf., pres.ind.pl., sjv., and pres.ptc.) appears in a few early 13th century MSS, which regularly have *-ie-* in short stems and *-i-* in long. But confusion soon sets in, and *-i-* gradually prevails.

PRETERITE

In the pret. and pret.ptc. the connecting vowel is regularly retained as *-e-*, and syncope only occurs in verbs with a long stem-vowel.

Note 6 *make(n)* has pret. *made* beside *maked*, pret.ptc. *ymaad*, *maad* beside *(i)maked(e)*.

CLASS 3

Present forms with geminates (i.e. inf., 1st pers. sg. and pl. ind., sjv., and ptc.) persist in the South into the 15th century; in the North and usually in the Midlands they are replaced by forms derived from the 2nd and 3rd pers. ind., which also appear in the South in the 14th century, for instance in Chaucer.

Thus: *libbe(n)* 'to live', N and later *liue(n)* and *leue* (with *ẹ* from *i* in an open syllable, §12, in the North, and *ẹ* from OE *leofast*, *leofaþ* in the South);

habbe(n) 'to have', later and N *haue(n)*, also *han*; 2nd sg. *hast*, N *has*; 3rd sg. *hath*, N *has*; pl. *haueth*, *haue(n)*, *han*, N *has*;

segge(n) 'to say', later and N *say*; etc.

§71 French Verbs

French verbs whose stem ends in a vowel (*-i*, *-ai*, or *-ei*) join class 1 of the weak verbs: e.g. *crye(n)* 'to cry', *assaye(n)* 'to try', and *obeie(n)* 'to obey'.

Those whose stem ends in a consonant are at first attached to weak verbs of class 2 in the South, and so keep in the present tense, where applicable, the endings *-ie-* ,*-i-*, and have no syncope of the vowel before *-d* in the pret. and pret.ptc.: hence *servi(n)* 'to serve', pret. *served*. In the North, and in the South after the loss of the distinctive endings of class 2, they are conjugated like all other weak verbs.

The Latin inchoative suffix *-iscis*, *-iscit* (which appears as *-ish* in ME, cf. §37B.2) is mostly taken to be part of the verb stem and maintained in all forms: hence *punishe(n)*, pret. and ptc. *punished*; but cf. *obeie(n)* 'to obey' and *sẹsen* 'to seize', without *-ish*.

The verb *strive(n)* 'to strive' (OF *estriver*) is conjugated as a class I strong verb, cf. §69, n. 3.

The verb *cacche(n)* 'to catch' forms its pret. and pret. ptc. *caught* on the model of class 1B of weak verbs, by analogy with OE *læċċean* 'to seize', pret. *læhte, lahte*.

§72   Preterite-Present Verbs

The forms preserved in ME are:

1. OE *wāt* 'know'

Inf. *wite(n)*, N also *wet*; pres. ind. 1st pers. *wāt*, S *wǫt*, also *ichot* with the pronoun; 2nd pers. *wāst, wǫst*; 3rd pers. *wāt, wǫt*; pl. *wite(n), witeþ*, Western *wuteþ, wuten*, N *wāt*; sjv. *wite, wite(n)*; imp. *wite*; pret. *wiste*, Western *wuste*.

2. OE *āh* 'possess'

Inf. *aghe, awe*, S *oʒe(n), owe(n)*; pres. ind. 1st and 3rd pers. N *agh, augh*, S *ough, ogh*; 2nd pers. N *aghte*, S *owest*; pl. N *aʒe, awe, agh*, S *owe(n)*; pret. N *aghte, aughte*, S *oughte, oghte*.

Note 1   From the 14th century the verb is conjugated as weak in the South; pres. ind. sg. *owe, owest*, pl. *oweþ, owe(n)*, pret. *owed*. In the North 3rd pers. sg. pres. *aweþ*, pret. *awed* also occur.

3. OE *dēag* 'avail'

Inf. *duʒen, dowe(n)*, 3rd pers. pres. sg. ind. *deigh*, in the 14th century *dow*, pl. *duʒen, dowen*; pret. *doughte, doghte*; from the 14th century, 3rd pers. pres. sg. ind. *dowes*, pret. *dowed*, in the North. Except in Scotland the verb later becomes obsolete.

4. OE *ann* 'grant'

Inf. *unnen, i-unnen*. The pres. ind. is conjugated weak: *unne, unnest, unneþ*, pl. *unneþ*; but 1st and 3rd pers. *an, on* also occur. The pret. is *ūþe*, the pret. ptc. *unnen, unned*. Found only in early S texts.

5. OE *cann* 'can, know'

Inf. *cun(nen), connen* (with *o* for *u*, §5B), N also *can*; pres. ind. 1st and 3rd pers. *can, con*; 2nd pers. *canst, cunst*; pl. *cunneþ*,

onneþ, cunne(n), conne(n), N *can, con;* pres.ptc. *cunninde, cun-*
,and, cunnyng; pret. *couþe* (with [ū]), from the 14th century
,lso coude.

6. OE *þearf* 'need'

Pres.ind.sg. 1st and 3rd pers. *þarf, þar;* 2nd pers. *þarft, þerft,*
,arst; pl. *þurve(n),* N and later also S *þarf, þar;* sjv. *þurve;* pret.
,orfte, þurte.

Note 2 Confusion with *dar* 'dare' is responsible both for forms with-
,ut *f* (or *v*) and for others with initial *d-* instead of *þ-.*

7. OE *dearr* 'dare'

Inf. *durre(n);* pres.ind.sg. 1st and 3rd pers. *dar, der;* 2nd pers.
,arst, derst, darist; pl. *durre(n), dor(ren),* N *der, dar;* sjv. *durre,*
N *dare;* pret. *durste, dorste.*

8. OE *sċeall* 'shall'

Pres.ind.sg. 1st and 3rd pers. *schal, schel;* 2nd pers. *schalt,*
,chult, schelt, N *schal;* pl. *schule(n), schollen,* N *schal;* sjv. *schulle;*
pret. *scholde, schulde.*

Note 3 In the North there are also forms with initial *s-* instead of
,ch-; cf. §38, n. 1.

9. OE *man* 'remember'

Inf. *munen, monen* (with *o* for *u,* §5B); pres.ind.sg. uniformly
,mun, mon; pl. *mune(n), mon;* sjv. *mune;* pret. *munde.* In the
North the pres. is also *man, mane.* The verb is uncommon everywhere.

10. OE *mæġ* 'may'

Inf. *muȝen, mowe(n);* pres.ind.sg. 1st and 3rd pers. *mai;* 2nd
pers. N *maght, maught,* later also *maist, mai,* S *might;* pl. *maȝe,*
mawe (OE *māgon), mai* (OE *mǣgon* or, in the North, modelled
on the sg.), *muȝe, mowe* (based on the inf.); sjv. *maȝe, mawe,*
mowe; pret. *mighte, moughte, mughte.*

11. OE *mōt* 'must'

Pres.ind.sg. 1st and 3rd pers. *moot, mōt;* 2nd pers. *most;* pl.
mōte(n); sjv *mōte;* pret. *moste, muste* (also used as a present
tense in the 15th century).

§73   The Substantive Verb ('to be')

PRESENT

Indicative

Singular: 1st person: *am* (OE *eam*), in early South Western texts also *eom, em* (OE *eom*); in early texts *beo, be*.

2nd person: S and M *art*; N *ert* (from ON *ert*), also *es, is* modelled on the 3rd person; *beest, best, bist*, South Western *bust* N *bes*.

3rd person: *is*; weak-stressed and in the East Midlands and North *es*; *beoþ, beþ, biþ*; South Western *buþ*, N *beis*.

Note 1   Forms of the pres.sg.ind. from the root **bheu* are common only in early texts; later only Scots *beis* remains, although Chaucer has 3rd person *beth* once. These forms, as already in OE, mostly have future meaning. *Best* and *beþ* are produced by analogy with the 1st person and the pl.

Plural: *ăre(n)* in the Midlands, the East Midlands particularly then in the North and in the 15th century also in London; *er* and without a pronoun also *es*, in the North. *Sinde(n), sunde(n)* occur only in the 13th century. *Beoþ, beþ*, in the Midlands later *be(n)*, are Southern and Midland until the 14th century, then only Southern and Western; in the North *beis* occurs only in Scotland, with future meaning.

Subjunctive (Optative)

Singular: *sie* (only in the South and Southwest until the 12th century); *beo, be* (generally); plural: *seon* (modelled on *beon*; only in isolated instances early in the South West); *beon, be(n)* (generally).

Imperative

Singular: *beo, be*; plural *beoþ, beþ, be(n)*, N *bees*. There is also *wes*, but this is found after 1200 only in the wish *wes heil* (ModE *wassail* 'good health!' as a toast).

Infinitive

   beon, be(n).

Participle

   N *beand(e)*, M and S later *beyng*.

PRETERITE

Indicative

Singular: 1st and 3rd pers. *was*, in Kent and sometimes elsewhere *wes*; 2nd pers. S *were*, M also *was*, N *was*; plural: *wēre(n)*, Eastern *wāre(n)*, in the East Midlands also *wōre*, N *war, wer* shortened as in §9.3).

Note 2 M *wore* and N *war* derive from ON *várom*.

Subjunctive

Singular: *were, ware, wore*; plural: *were(n), ware, wore*.

Participle

ibe(n), bee(n).

§74 The Verb 'to will'

Pres. ind.: sg.: 1st and 3rd pers. *wille, wil*, M also *welle*, S and W *wule* (with [ü]), later also *wole(n)* (with [u] from [ü] as in 11.5, or with [o] from the pret.); 2nd pers. *wilt, wult, wolt*; pl.: *willeþ, woleþ*, M *wille(n), wol(l)en, wolle*, N *will, welyn, wol(l)e(n)*.
Sjv.: sg.: *wille, wulle, wole*; pl.: *wille(n), wulle(n), wole(n)*.
Inf.: *willen, will*.
Pret.: *wolde, wulde*, N and W *walde*.
Pret. Ptc.: *wold*.

Note Negative forms have initial *n-* (*nill*, etc.). No present negative forms with *-o-* are found.

§75 The Verb 'to do'

Pres. ind.: sg.: 1st pers. *do*; 2nd *dost*, N *dos*, S also *dest*; 3rd *doþ, dos*, S and eME also *deþ*; pl.: S *doþ*, M *do(n)*, N *dos*.
Sjv.: sg. *do*, pl. *do(n)*.
Imp.: sg. *do*, pl. *doþ, do(n)*, N *dos*.
Pres. ptc.: S *doinde*, M *doende*, N *doande*; S and M later *doing*.
Inf.: *do(n)*.
Pret.: S and W *dude* (with [ü]), Kt *dede*, M and N *dide, dede* with lengthening as in §12B).
Pret. ptc.: *ido, don*.
This verb *do(n)* is also used as an auxiliary with the infinitive of another verb as causative and intensive; in the latter use it is often quite pleonastic, particularly in poetry, where it is a handy

way of filling up a line. The use of expressions containing *do* ir
questions and negative sentences did not develop until ModE
where these occur in ME, they are to be taken as intensive o1
pleonastic.

§76   The Verb 'to go'

In OE there were two verbs, *gān* and *gangan*; after the 14tl
century, forms derived from the latter remain only in Scotland

Pres. ind.: sg.: 1st pers. *gā*, *gǭ* (cf. §11.4); 2nd *gāst*, *gǭst*, ir
early S texts also *gēst*, N *gās*; 3rd S *gǭþ*, in earlier texts also *gēþ*
N *gās*; pl.: S *gǭþ*, M *gǭ(n)*, *gān*, *gā*, N *gās*, *gǭs* (in border-areas
or due to dialect-mixture).

Sjv.: sg. *gā*, *gǭ*; pl. *gā*, *gǭ(n)*.

Pres. Ptc.: *gǭinde*, *gǭende*, North Midland *gǭande*, N *gangande*
Inf.: *gā*, *gǭ(n)*.

Pret.: *eode*, *ode*, *ede* in the South in the 12th century; S alsɔ
ʒ*eode* (from *geēode*), Eastern ʒ*ede*, later in the S and M ʒ*ede*, ʒ*ode*
also ʒ*edd*, ʒ*odd*; and in the N from 1400 *gaed*, newly formed fron
the inf. The forms ʒ*ede*, ʒ*ode* die out in the South in the 15tl
century, being replaced by *went*, derived from *wenden* 'to mak
one's way, to walk', which is almost synonymous with *go* alread
in Chaucer.

Pret. ptc.: *igǭ(n)*, *gǭ(n)*, N *gān*, *gain* (cf. §5, n. 5).

§77   Compound Tenses

1. PERFECT

To refer to an action in the past, OE possessed, as well as th
preterite, a perfect tense—consisting of the present of the ver
'to be' or of *habban* with a pret. ptc.—which signified an actiɔ
that, although past, has some reference to the present.

The two forms, preterite and perfect, were not yet, howevei
as sharply differentiated as they are now, and the preterite wa
sometimes used in OE even when the action had an undoubte
reference to the present. In ME it still occurs, particularly i
the Wycliffite Bible, where it is used to translate perfect tense
in the Latin, e.g. *What to me and to the, womman, myn our cai
not ʒit* (Lat. *nondum venit*; AV *is not com*), and in Chaucer, aftɛ
sith, as in *By this gaude have I wonne, yeer by yeer, an hundre
mark sith I was pardoner* and *What I haue suffred sith I was a wyf
Conversely, the perfect is used (although rarely) for an actiɔ

completed in the past, e.g. *This world is nat so strong, it is no nay, As it hath been of olde tymes yoore* (C).

To form the perfect, the present of *habbe(n)*, *have* is used with transitive verbs and the verb 'to be'; with intransitive verbs, the present of the verb 'to be' is used, save that with verbs of motion and rest *habbe(n)*, *have* is also found (although less often) when the emphasis is upon the action itself rather than the fact that it is concluded. Examples are: *He took his wyf to kepe whan he is gon* compared with *and also to han gon to solitarie exil*, or *the yonge sonne hath in the Ram his halfe cours yronne* compared with *as rody and bright as dooth the yonge sonne that in the Ram 's foure degrees up ronne* (all C).

2. PLUPERFECT

This tense is formed in ME in a way similar to the perfect, i.e. by adding to a pret. ptc. the pret. of *habbe(n)*, *have*, or of the verb 'to be'. In subordinate clauses the preterite is also used occasionally to denote the anterior past, as it still is in ModE; an example is *When tyme cam, men thoughte it for the beste that evel stynte* (C).

3. FUTURE

OE, like other Gmc languages, had no future tense, and almost always used in its stead (e.g. to translate Latin future tenses) the pres. ind. In ME, from about the 12th century, a construction consisting of the present of the verb 'shall' (*schal*, etc.) and an infinitive is increasingly used to indicate a future action, as in *ich schal heom singe and sitte bi* (*The Owl and the Nightingale*) and *To love my lady, whom I love and serve and ever shal, til that myn herte sterve* (C), alongside the present, and also expressions employing *mot*, *mun*, and *will*, which are infrequent; those with *will* do become commoner about 1400, but nearly always retain the sense of volition, as in *I wil araise and auntre it* (C).

Note 1 The construction with *shall* can, however, still refer to an obligation, as in *Lat se now who shal telle the firste tale* (C, Prologue to the *Canterbury Tales*, 831, before the draw is made).

Note 2 *Will* in *Oure manciple I hope he will be deed* (*Reeve's Tale*, 4029) is probably a pure future; if so, it is the only instance in Chaucer.

Note 3 There are very few instances of a secondary future ('Futurum Exactum') in ME, but it is found here and there, constructed with

shall, inf. *have*, and a pret.ptc., as in *I shall han chaunged* (C, Boec
V 1920, for Lat. *mutavero*).

Note 4   ME forms a conditional with *sholde*, as in *ʒif schrift schuld*
hit thenne swopen out, a gret wonder hit were (Langland).

§78   The Passive Voice

In OE the passive is formed by combining the verb *weorþan*
or the verb 'to be' with a pret.ptc. There seems to be no par
ticular distinction of meaning between the two constructions
that with *weorþan* becomes less common in later OE and i
gradually dropped in ME.

Originally a personal passive is only possible with verbs whicl
take an object in the accusative; in the passive constructioi
this becomes the subject. Already in ME there are some earl
instances of passive constructions with a personal subject whicl
would have been dative in an active construction, e.g. *Ure lover*
beo iðonked (Ancren Riwle; in another MS we find *Ure loverd hi*
beo iðonked, in which *Ure loverd* is probably to be regarded as a
uninflected dative); *This child I am comaunded for to take* (C
beside *What was comaunded unto Lamuel* (C); but this sort c
construction does not become fully developed and in general us
until early in ModE.

§79   The Periphrastic Verb Conjugation

This is fully developed (as *I am singing*, etc.) only in the 17t
and 18th centuries. In ME, particularly in the North and Scot
land, constructions consisting of the verb 'to be' and the pre
ptc. are used quite commonly with verbs of motion and rest t
emphasise the action of the verb, e.g. *When þe Emperiz her*
tiþand þat þe childe was . . . cumand (*Seven Sages*, Northern ver
sion), but the simple form of the verb is mostly used in suc
cases. In the South constructions of this kind are seldom ev
denced while the pres.ptc. and the verbal noun have differer
forms (cf. §68), and those consisting of the verb 'to be' or othe
verbs with the verbal noun in *-ing* or *-ung*, preceded by th
preposition *on* or *in*, occur rather more often than in the Nort
(e.g. *he was on huntyng, þis chirch was in bylding*). After th
coincidence in form of the pres.ptc. and the verbal noun, th
construction consisting of the verb 'to be' and a form in *-in*
without a preposition, is found quite commonly to express
continuing action, although not invariably. Examples ar

yngynge he was or floytynge al the day; *Whilom ther was dwellynge
n Lumbardye*; and (to indicate something customary) *This somo-
.our that was as ful of jangles . . . And ever enqueryng upon every
.hing*. The use of this construction rather than the simple verb
s perhaps due, especially in poetry, to reasons of metre and
·hythm.

§80   The Infinitive and the Gerund

1. THE INFINITIVE

This form—originally a verbal abstract, transferred to the
·onjugation of the verb—is rarely subject of a verb in OE,
·ut often object, both by itself and with another object. As the
·omplement of adjectives, participles and some verbs (especially
·hose with an impersonal subject), the infinitive has the prep.
·ō, and in OE is regularly found in the inflected form *-anne, -enne*
which disappears in eME, §68, n. 7).

Towards the end of the OE period the simple infinitive (with-
·ut *tō*) appears less and less, and in ME it is found very rarely
·xcept after verbs of sense-perception, preterite-presents, and
·erbs specifying a type of action, such as *do, ginne(n), let* etc.
·lsewhere, and in its ME use as a subject, the infinitive is pre-
·eded by *to* or *for to*, to express the aim or purpose more clearly.

ME thus has: *Horn gan for to ride*; *þe se bigan to flowe*; or (with
nf. as subject) *betere þe is freondscipe to habben þene for to fihten*
Laȝamon); *To tellen al wolde passen any bible* (C); (inf. without
·) *That stinteth first whan she biginneth singe* (C); but also: *Gan
·n a Troyen lay to singen clere* (C); (after verbs of sense-percep-
ion) *I sawe come with a glad chere to me a lusty bachelere* and
·Vhan Palamon the larke herde synge* (C).

Note 1   In Northern texts *til(l)* is found instead of *to*, cf. §42.3.

2. THE GERUND

The verbal abstract (*-ung, -ing* in OE) competes extensively
·vith the infinitive. In origin it is purely substantival, but in
·IE it is increasingly transferred to the verb inflexion, partly
·ecause of its coalescence with the pres. ptc. (see §68). The fact
·hat in the course of ME it came to be taken as verbal can be
·een in the following: (1) its being used without an article, where
· noun would have one, e.g. *For to be wys in byynge of vitaille* (C);

G

and (2) its appearance with a complement which is in the objec case, not in the genitive, as in *take him þe keping þe coroun* or *he comaundit his knightis for keping the yatis* (*Destructio of Troy*), or *In lifting up his hevy dronken cors* (C); althoug expressions like *in kepyng of thy persone* (C) and *in yevynge o wikked conseil* (C) remain commoner in ME.

Being verbal, forms in -*ing* can be used (in the manner o Latin gerunds) as the complement of a verb, like the infinitiv with *to*: hence *He kan nat stynte of syngyng by the waye besid repentant folk that stynte for to synne* (both C).

Note 1   Before the use of forms in -*ing*, Latin gerunds were translate by infinitives with *tō* or by the pres. ptc.: OE *god hǣle tō dōnne* (in th Psalter, *Deus salvos faciendi*) and *tīd tō miltsiende him* (*tempus miserand eius*).

The use of the pres. ptc. as a gerund (which was common in French is encouraged in the South by its coalescence with the verbal noun i -*ing*, but this use is found also in the North, where the coalescence di not take place.

Note 2   After verbs of sense-perception with a personal object (wher the infinitive is also found, as in *They sawe hym sette on lofte*, C) forms i -*ing* are to be interpreted as present participles, e.g. *and sawe folk in th way passyng* (C) or Northern *He saʒe þam in þe hiʒe see sailand togedir*

INDEX

The numbers refer to articles (§§), not pages.
Note that:

   (i) *ʒ* is entered under *y*;
   (ii) *y* denoting a vowel is disregarded, and *i* is used;
   (iii) *sch* and *sh* are both put under *sch*;
   (iv) *th* or *ð* replacing *þ* are entered under the latter, which appears between *t* and *u*;
   (v) initial *v* and *u* are not distinguished.

The form closest to that current in Modern English is used as the main heading for each word; under it are placed references to all the Middle English forms of the word. Verbs appear under the infinitive.

A

_ see *he* or *sche* pers. pron.
_ see *one* num.
_- prefix 30
_bbot n. 24
_boute prep. 30
_che v. 21.2
_cht see *eight* num.
_dde(n) v. 21.3
_drad p.p. 30
_dreint p.p. 13D.3
_ffaire n. 22B.5
_ffere see *affaire* n.
_gain adv. 30
_ge n. 31, n.2; 38.2
_gh 1.3 sg. of *owe(n)* v.
_ghe inf. see *owe(n)* v.
_ght see *eight* or *eighthe* num.
_ghte pret. of *owe(n)* v.
_i n. 13A.3; 42
_ir n. 22B.5
_iper see *eiper* pron.
_ker, -ir n. 26
_ld see *old* adj.
_lder see *aller* adj. gen.pl.
_lder cpv.adj. 10, n. 1, para. 2
_le n. 11.1
_ller adj. gen.pl. 43
_llerbest spv.adj. 43

allermost spv.adj. 43
am 1 pres.sg. of *be* 73
amonge prep. 8; 11, n.16; 30
amorous adj. 21.5
an indef.art. 34; 49.1
an 1.3 pres.sg. of *unnen* v.
an, aan see *one* num. and indef. pron.
-and see *-ing*
anes see *ones* adv.
angel n. 22B.1
anne acc. of *an* see *one* num.
anoon adv. 30
-ant, -aunt 68, n.9
any pron. 11, n.9; 62
appel, n. 11.1
apt adj. 21.3
ar adv. 16
are dat.fem. of *one* num.
are(n) pl. of *be* 73
arm n. 11.1
arme n. 21.3
art 2 sg.pres. of *be* 73
ask v., pret. *asked, -id* 24, n. 3; 38.1
assai n. 22B.5
assaile(n), assalʒe(n) v. 22B.7 and n.7
assaye(n) v. 71
at pl. *ate(n)*, pret. of *ete(n)* v.

attend v. 68, n.3

auchtande see *eighthe* num.

augh 1.3 sg.pres. of *owe(n)* v.

aught pron. 64

aught see *eight* num.

aughte pret. of *owe(n)* v.

aungel see *angel* n.

aunter, -ir see *aventure* n.

auþer see *eiþer* pron.

aventure n. 31B

avoir n. 22, n.5

awede pret. of *owe(n)* v.

awen inf. see *owe(n)* v.

axe(n) see *ask* v.

aȝen, aȝhenn see *own* adj.

aȝthe see *eighthe* num.

B

ba see *boþe* num.

bacoun n. 21.2

baien inf. see *bui(en)* v.

baieþ ȝ.sg of *bui(en)* v.

bain see *bon* n.

bak n. 11.1 and n.2

bame n. 22, n.2

ban see *bon* n.

band see *bond* n.

bar, bare(n) pret. see *bere(n)* v.

baron, -oun n. 21.2

basin n. 21.2

bataile, batalȝe n. 20; 22B.7

baþe see *boþe* num.

bathe v. 12A

be, beon inf. 73

beand pres.ptc. see *beyng*

Beauchamp see *Becham*

Beaumont see *Bemont*

Becham 22, n.2; 23.8

beck n. 21.4

bede(n) v. 69, n.7

beef n. 23.3

bee(n) pret.ptc. of *be* 73

beet pret. of *bete(n)* v.

begge(n) inf. see *bui(en)* v.

beggers pl.n. 28

beginnen v. 38, n.9

beie see *boþe* num.

beien inf. see *bui(en)* v.

beis pres.pl. of *be* 73

bek see *beck* n.

bek see *bak* n.

Bemont 23.8

beoþ pres. and imp.pl. of *be* 73

berd 'beard' n. 35

berd 'bird' see *bird* n.

bere(n) v.; pret. *ba(a)r*, *boor*, pl *bare(n)*, *booren*; p.p. *bor(e)n* 12A 28; 29B.2; 69.IV and n.9

bert see *berd* n. 'beard'

best 2 pres.sg. of *be* 73

beste n. 22A

bet, beot pret. of *bete(n)* v.

bet, better cpv.adj. 45; 47; 56, n.3

bete(n) v. 69 and n.23

beþ 3 sg. and pl.ind., and imp.pl of *be* 73

beyng pres.ptc. of *be* 73

bi- prefix 30

bidde(n) v. 69, n.7

bie inf. see *bui(en)* v.

bieþ see *bui(en)* v.

bifore prep. 12A; 30

bigge(n) inf. see *bui(en)* v.

bindeth, -ith 3 sg.pres. of *binde(n* 24, n.3

birch n. 38.1

bird n. 11, n.16; 33, n.

birden see *burden* n.

birk see *birch* n.

biseech v. 38.1

bishop n. 24

bist 2 sg.pres. of *be* 73

bitt 3 sg.pres. of *bite(n)* v. 68, n. 3

biþ 3 sg.pres. of *be* 73

black adj. 11, n.2; 12C.3; 38.1

blame v. 21.2

blew pret. of *blowe(n)* v. 'to blow'

bloome n. 17

blowe(n), blawe(n) v. 'to blow' 13B.2 and n.7; 69.VII

blowe(n) v. 'to bloom' 13B.4

bo see *boþe* num.

bodi n., pl. *bodies* 12C

bogh see *bough* n.

bon, boon n. 11.4; 13D.1

bond n. 17

fischers pl. n. 28

five num. 36; 49.5

flank n. 22B.1

flat adj. 17

flee(n) v. 69.2

fleie(n) see *flie(n)* v.

fleigh pret. of *flee(n)* or *flie(n)* v. 69, n. 5

fle(i)sch n. 13D.3; 36

flew pret. of *flie(n)* v.

flie(n) v. 69, n. 5

flour n. 22B.4

flowen p.p. of *flee(n)* v.

flowe(n) v. 69.VII and n. 23

flozen p.p. of *flee(n)* v.

fluzen pl. pret. of *flee(n)* v.

foghten p.p. of *fighte(n)*

fol see *ful* adj.

folde(n) v. 69.VII, pret. *feeld*

fon see *fange(n)* v.

fond sg. pret. of *finde(n)* v.

fonge(n) see *fange(n)* v.

fool n. 22A

foot n. 42.5C

for, foor sg., *foren* pl. pret. of *fare(n)* v.

for to with inf. 80.1

forlees sg., *forlore* pl. pret. of *forlese(n)* v.

forlese(n), forleose(n) v. 29B.2; 69.2

forlorne p.p. of *forlese(n)* v.

forlure(n) pl. pret. of *forlese(n)* v.

forme, cpv. *former,* spv. *formest* num. 50

forþi see *þe* dem. pron. 56, n. 3

forʒeten v. 38, n. 9

foul see *fowl* n.

found pl. pret. of *finde(n)* v.

four num. 13, n. 6 and n. 9; 29B.1; 49.4

fourscore num. 49.80

fourte see *fourþe* num.

fourti num. 49.40

fourþe num. 50

fower see *four* num.

fowerti see *fourti* num.

fowl n. 13B.5; 42.5A

fowles pl. n. 42.5A

fra see *fro* prep.

fraine n. 37B.3

freese(n) v., pret. *frees* 69.2

frere n. 11, n. 19

fresh adj. 33, n.; 38.1

freut see *fruit* n.

frigid adj. 21.2

frist see *firste* num.

fro prep. 17

frogge n. 38.2

front n. 22B.3

froren, frosen p.p. of *freese(n)* v.

fruit n. 23.6

frunt see *front* n.

frusshe(n) v. 37B.2

frut see *fruit* n.

ful adj. 11, n. 16

funden p.p. of *finde(n)* v.

fur see *fir* n.

furde see *fourþe* num.

furst see *firste* num.

fuwer see *four* num.

G

ga inf. see *go(n)* v.

gaed pret. of *go(n)* v.

gail see *jail* n.

gailer see *jailer* n.

gain p.p. of *go(n)* v.

gain(nen), ganʒe v. 22B.7 and n. 7

galwe n. 26

gan, gon pl. pres. and p.p. of *go(n)* v.

gangande pres. ptc. of *go(n)* v.

gardin n. 38.2

gas 3 sg. and pl. pres. of *go(n)* v.

gast, gost 2 sg. pres. of *go(n)* v.

gauk = gouk n.

gentel, gentil adj. 31B

gers see *grass* n.

gest n. 17; 38, n. 9

gest 2.3 sg. pres. of *go(n)*

geste n. 38.2

gete(n) v. 12, n. 2; 38, n. 9; 69, n. 15

geten, goten p.p. of *gete(n)* v.

geþ, goþ 3 sg. pres. of *go(n)* v.

gewis 3 sg. pres. of *give(n)* 32, n. 1

gide see *guide* n.

giffis 3 sg. pres. of *give(n)* v. 36, n. 3

Y